D1452423

BEYOND PORT AND PREJUDICE

Charles Lloyd
Canon of Christ Church
Regius Professor of Divinity
Bishop of Oxford
1784–1829

BEYOND
PORT AND PREJUDICE

Charles Lloyd
of Oxford, 1784-1829

William J. Baker

Illustrations by Arline K. Thomson

University of Maine at Orono Press
Orono, Maine 1981

Manufactured in the United States of America

First edition

Library of Congress Card Catalog Number: 76-24243

ISBN 0-89101-032-7

1 2 3 4 5 6 7 8 9

For TINA and DAVID,
to whom,
in different ways,
I am indebted.

CONTENTS

ILLUSTRATIONS

PREFACE

That there are men of learning in the University of Oxford competent to a great undertaking . . ., we can scarcely allow ourselves to doubt; and happy should we be to rouse their industry and stimulate their ambition, so as to make them shake off the benumbing influence of port and prejudice, — do themselves and their country honour, and the republic of letters essential service.
— Edinburgh Review, 1809.

SEVERAL RECENT ATTEMPTS at historical revision notwithstanding, "the benumbing influence of port and prejudice" was everywhere evident at Oxford University in the second half of the eighteenth century. Even more than Cambridge, Oxford had become a haven of aristocratic privilege and academic lethargy. Heads of colleges were concerned primarily with ecclesiastical controversy and ministerial politics, indolent tutors scarcely bothered to teach, portly professors seldom gave evidence of any original scholarship, and undergraduates made little pretence of intellectual ambition. Social status and conviviality mattered most in the academic *ancien régime*.

By the turn of the nineteenth century, however, a new era was appearing. As England changed rapidly from a rural to an urban society, from an agricultural to an industrial economy, Oxford resisted but could not prevent the winds of change from blowing down its narrow streets and through its courtyards. Protected by ancient charters and hallowed traditions, dons young and old continued to be involved in daily rounds of leisurely conversation and wearisome debates on the nature of the Church and the prospects of governmental ministries. But they were forced, by pressures internal as well as external, to attend to educational priorities. Not yet devoted to much research and scholarly penmanship, they nevertheless renewed the University's historic commitment to serious study and intellectual engagement. A concerned, ambitious, industrious new breed of Oxford don emerged in the early years of the nineteenth century.

Charles Lloyd exemplified that new breed. When he matriculated at Christ Church in 1803, Lloyd labored under a double disadvantage. The son of a poor clergyman, he lacked connections as well as wealth; having come from Eton, he soon learned that position and honor at Christ Church were normally reserved for Old Westminsters. These difficulties merely fired his ambition to excel. Within his first year he was granted a Studentship, and in 1806 he achieved highest honors in his examinations. After a year's absence from the University, he returned to Christ Church to perform admirably as a mathematics lecturer and tutor until 1819, filling several important college offices in the process. Firmly based in the Christ Church world of influence and patronage, he successfully sought the appointment as the Preacher of Lincoln's Inn (1819); in 1822 he returned yet again to Christ Church, this time as a Canon and Regius Professor of Divinity; in 1827 he became the Bishop of Oxford. Most importantly, from his Regius chair he achieved a remarkable awakening of interest in theological studies at the University. Organs of contemporary opinion as diverse as the *Times,* the *Edinburgh Review,* and the *Quarterly Review* lauded his efforts. A recent historian of nineteenth century Oxford rightly refers to him as "the most influential Oxford professor of his day."[1]

Yet he has been virtually ignored. Not an author of any significance, Lloyd left few printed words through which he might posthumously impress the reading public. Nor did his family or friends honor him with a biography. Information on his life and work has been scattered, based largely on the published correspondence of his more famous pupils (such as Robert Peel) or the reminiscences of Oxford graduates who were primarily intent on explaining their own involvement in, or opposition to, the Oxford Movement of the 1830's and '40's.

Although Lloyd died four years before the first "Tract for the Times" was published, he contributed greatly to the doctrinal origins of the Oxford Move-

1. W.R. Ward, *Victorian Oxford* (1965), p. 52

ment. In public lectures and private classes he introduced John Henry Newman, E. B. Pusey, Hurrell Froude, Frederick Oakeley, and many less famous young men to the treasures of the Anglican heritage, training them theologically for their bold assertion of the ancient doctrines and autonomy of the Church of England. Personifying what David Newsome refers to as a "peculiar buoyancy and zest" which characterized the University in the 1820's, Lloyd helped to transform Gibbon's Oxford into Newman's Oxford. This book is about that transformation as it was represented in Lloyd's efforts in "fostering a spirit and devising techniques" which were to have "cataclysmic effects" on the intellectual and religious life of Victorian England.[2].

Like most practitioners of Clio's craft, I have incurred numerous debts of gratitude. A generous grant from the American Philosophical Society made possible the initial research; a summer research grant from the University of Maine at Orono enabled me to complete the project. In correspondence and personal conversations I have received information (and, of equal importance, encouragement) from Professors Owen Chadwick, Hugh Lloyd-Jones, Frederick Shriver, Geoffrey Best, H. J. Hanham, Richard Davis, and Burton Throckmorton, the late George Kitson Clark, and the present Earl of Elgin.

For their unfailing cooperation in my use of unpublished manuscripts at their disposal, I am grateful to Dr. J. F. A. Mason and his assistant librarian, H. J. R. Wing, at Christ Church; Miss Molly Barratt and her colleagues at the Bodleian; the late Father Stephen Dessain at the Birmingham Oratory; James

---

2.   David Newsome, *The Parting of Friends: A Study of the Wilberforces and Henry Manning* (1966), p. 62.

Lawson at Shrewsbury School; the Keeper of Western Manuscripts and his staff at the British Museum;
J. D. Makepeace and P. G. Cobb of Pusey House,
Oxford; the archivists at the Buckinghamshire
County Record Office, Aylesbury; E. G. W. Bill at
Lambeth Palace Library; Ian C. A. Bowles of Magdalen College, Oxford; and M. B. Parkes at Keble College, Oxford. The research for this book could not
have been completed, much less made pleasant, without their cordial assistance.

Early drafts of the typescript were read critically by
David Newsome, my former Cambridge doctoral
supervisor, now Headmaster of Christ's Hospital in
Sussex; Peter Stansky of Stanford University; Piers
Brendon, W. R. Carr, and James Axtell, friends and
kind critics all. The present text is vastly different
from those earlier versions, largely because of the
helpful comments of these fellow historians. Several
colleagues at the University of Maine at Orono —
notably Edward Holmes, James Miller, Jerome
Nadelhaft, David Smith, Robert Thomson, and Margaret Danielson — assisted me in preparing the
typescript for the press.

Dr. J. F. A. Mason of Christ Church was especially
helpful. He carefully scanned the text for errors,
gaps in the Christ Church basis of the story, and
infelicities which might have jarred English, if not
American, readers. Had it not been for his queries
and suggestions, the book would have been published
much earlier but less satisfactorily. His interest in the
subject prompted him to extend his librarian's skills
in a search for additional unpublished manuscripts.
Just as the book was going to the printers, he discovered five letters from Lloyd to H. H. Norris, 1827-28,
which were purchased recently by the Bodleian Lib-

rary from the S.P.C.K.; eighteen letter from Lloyd to
Thomas Gaisford, 1816-28, in the private collection
of the Gaisford-St. Lawrence family at Howth Castle,
Dublin; and two dozen or so miscellaneous items pertaining to Lloyd's private affairs, which are in the
personal possession of Mr. David Sanctuary Howard.
Unfortunately, copies of these letters and papers
reached me too late to be incorporated in this book.
Several passages would have buttressed various
points and added color to the narrative, but none
could contradict the central argument.

The editors of the *Huntington Library Quarterly*
kindly granted me permission to use the material in
the second chapter, which originally appeared in a
slightly different form in their journal. Finally, and
most of all, I am grateful to Tina, my wife, who
cheerfully encouraged and faithfully endured my
prolonged affair with Charles Lloyd.

W.J.B.
Bangor, Maine
1981

Author's Note: For convenience I have used the spelling of Lloyd's surname by which he is normally
known, but there can be no doubt that the man himself
used the spelling LLoyd, as indeed his descendants still
do.

ABBREVIATIONS OF MANUSCRIPT COLLECTIONS

The following abbreviations are used for manuscripts cited often in the footnotes:

BM Add. MS.   — British Museum,*
                      Peel Papers

Oratory MS.   — Birmingham Oratory,
                      Froude Letters

Bodl. MS. ODP — Bodleian Library,
                      Oxford Diocesan Papers

Ch. Ch. MS.   — Christ Church Archives,
                      Chinnery Correspondence

Pusey MS.   — Pusey House (Oxford),
                      Pusey Papers

Shrewsbury   — Shrewsbury School Library,
  School MS.   Burton Letters

Other manuscripts are given complete reference in the footnotes.

All books cited were published in London, unless otherwise indicated.

*This traditional designation has been changed recently to the British Library.

BEYOND PORT AND PREJUDICE

I ETON AND CHRIST CHURCH

THE ERA OF CHARLES LLOYD'S BIRTH and early childhood was described by Dickens as "the best of times,...the worst of times." In the last quarter of the eighteenth century wisdom and foolishness, civility and barbarity, belief and incredulity, opulence and poverty existed side by side in England, glaringly juxtaposed. Tensions resulting from these contradictions required the established orders to create both the mechanisms and the myth of stability. While "a king with a large jaw and a queen with a plain face" sat on the throne of England, it appeared "clearer than crystal to the lords of the state preserves of loaves and fishes, that things in general were settled for ever."[1]

Society was settled, but not stagnant. In 1784, the year of Lloyd's birth, young William Pitt consolidated his position as the leader of a newly-invigorated Tory party set on healing the old breach between Commons and King. As George III himself anticipated "a firm, efficient, extended, united administration,"[2] moderate reform was the order of the day. But portents of more radical change were present. In a parliamentary election in April, 1784, a diminutive, wealthy, but unknown Tory was returned for Yorkshire: William Wilberforce, not yet converted to Evangelicalism, knowing little and caring less about the slave trade, was launching a political career in which the humanitarian impulses of a new age were to be embodied. Other notable portents were less public. In 1784 Peter Onions and Henry Cort patented their "puddling process" for the large-scale conversion of pig iron into tougher wrought iron, James Watt perfected a device by which his steam engine could turn a wheel, and Edmund Cartwright was hard at work on a mechanical loom. English life was scarcely to remain "settled for ever" in its old rural, aristocratic patterns.

Far removed from the centers of political reform and industrial change, Charles Lloyd was born on September 26, 1784, in the little village of West Wycombe, Buckinghamshire. He was the second

1. This reference is, of course, from the opening page of Dickens' *Tale of Two Cities*, originally published in 1859. For the best general histories of late eighteenth century England, see J. Steven Watson, *The Reign of George III 1760-1815* (Oxford, 1960), and Asa Briggs, *The Age of Improvement 1783-1867* (1959).

2. *The Annual Register, or a View of the History, Politics, and Literature for the Years 1784 and 1785* (1800, 2nd ed.), p. 310.

son, the third of seven children, of Thomas and Elizabeth Lloyd. His father, a curate in the church at West Wycombe since 1773, was Oxford-educated and socially respected; but his annual stipend amounted to only £66 per year. To supplement his income, Thomas Lloyd tutored private pupils, a common practice for poorly-paid but energetic clergymen in the eighteenth century, when England's old 'public' (i.e. private) schools were unruly, and no universal public education was yet available.[3]

Within a year of Charles' birth, the Lloyd family moved to nearby Bradenham.The father continued serving his curacy at West Wycombe, a few miles away, but increasingly put most of his energy into the supervision of his private pupils. In addition to teaching children who lived in the immediate vicinity, he boarded and taught children from some of the "highest families in the country."Apparently his quarters soon became cramped, for after a few years at Bradenham, he moved his family and pupils to take up tenancy on Lord Dormer's estate just outside Great Missenden. There the elder Lloyd lived until his death in 1815, teaching his own children as well as his private pupils the rudiments of Latin and Greek, classical literature, mathematics, and some history; and drilling them in the reading, writing, and speaking of Italian as well as French.[4]

3. MS. copies of Parish Registers, Buckinghamshire County Record Office: D/A/T 197 (West Wycombe) and D/A/T/ 23 (Bradenham); MS. Disbursement Book of Richard Levett [Lloyd's vicar], Buckinghamshire County Record Office. On the clergyman as private tutor, see John Lawson and Harold Silver, *A Social History of Education in England* (1973), pp. 202-3.

4. *The Gentleman's Magazine and Historical Chronicle,* XCIX (1829), 560-61.

The fruit of Thomas Lloyd's pedagogical efforts
was to be seen in the achievements of three of his
four sons. Thomas, Charles, and William Forster all
won scholarships to Eton. It was said of young
Thomas that he ran "a course as brilliant as ever was
granted by Providence to boy" before his sudden
death at Eton in 1800. Charles and William Forster
went on to win Studentships at Christ Church, Oxford, where Charles later became the Regius
Professor of Divinity and William Forster became
the Drummond Professor of Political Economy. The
Lloyds' father laid firm academic foundations.[5]

Although the father lived to be 70 and the mother
54 years of age, most of the Lloyd children were not
physically strong. The first two daughters died in in-
fancy; Thomas lived to be only 18, and another son,
Edward, was chronically ill throughout his life. In
that day when smallpox was a killer, when cholera
was still a plague on mankind, and when even a
common cold often led to pneumonia and quick
death, a "weak constitution" precluded much hope
for a long life. Charles Lloyd's relatively early death
is best viewed within the light of his family's unenvi-
able medical history.

His later religious perspective, too, was in keeping
with the pattern established in his home. Religion,
for the Lloyds, was reasonable and prosaically orthodox. Thomas Lloyd had no sympathy whatsoever
for the Biblical dogmatism and revivalistic enthusiasm associated with sectarian Dissent; nor was
he inclined to look favorably upon that recent group
of insurgents within the Church of England, the

---

5. *Ibid.; Dictionary of National Biography*, XXXIII, 411; for information
   on William Forster Lloyd, see *D.N.B.*, XXXIII, 440.

Evangelicals. The traditional place of the creeds and the customary use of the Prayer Book were unquestioned. For the Lloyds, as for one of their contemporaries, "Christianity had wrought itself into the constitution of their natures. It was a necessary part of the existing order of the universe, as little to be debated about as the movements of the planets or the changes of the seasons."[6]

Politically the Lloyds were Whigs.[7] But for Whigs and Tories alike, the single most important event affecting Charles Lloyd's generation was the French Revolution. As young Lloyd approached his fifth birthday, the French Revolution began as a moderate reform movement. English liberals (many of whom were Whigs) applauded, formed supporting societies, and wrote pamphlets urging similar reforms in Britain. Then the French scene turned radically violent. Aristocratic homes were sacked, Church property was confiscated, and in January, 1793, Louis XVI was sent to the guillotine. British opinion soured quickly. As a few English radicals continued to rail against landlords, the Church, and the monarchy, a fear of Jacobins swept across the country. Repressive legislation was enacted. In 1792 a proclamation was issued against "seditious writings"; in 1794 *habeas corpus* was suspended, and in 1795 the Treasonable and Seditious Practices Act and the Seditious Assemblies Act were passed. Much

6. J.A. Froude, *Short Studies on Great Subjects,* 4 vols. (1897), IV, 243. Froude insisted that his household was "a fair representative of the [old] order" (p. 241).

7. I am grateful to Professor Richard Davis of Washington University (St. Louis) for this information, uncovered in his research on Buckinghamshire politics. See his *Political Change and Continuity, 1760-1885: A Buckinghamshire Study* (Newton Abbot, 1972).

of Charles Lloyd's youth was spent in a national atmosphere of frantic reaction.[8]

With his family a part of the established order of
church and landed interest, Lloyd's social and
political principles flowed naturally in a conservative
vein. The French Revolution served to confirm that
tendency. Like his older, illustrious neighbor, Edmund Burke, Lloyd developed a "powerful pre-
possession towards antiquity." Tradition, not
abstract theory, would be his ideal; gradual improvement, not radical alteration, would be his goal.
When Burke argued that "the idea of inheritance
furnishes a sure principle of conservatism, and sure
principle of transmission; without at all excluding a
principle of improvement," he spoke prophetically
for Lloyd's generation.[9] Not until the 1820's would
the "principle of improvement" cease being an af-
terthought for Lloyd.

But if his conservatism can be traced, in part, to a
reaction against the French Revolution, his liberal
attitudes towards Roman Catholicism can also be attributed to the effects of that continental upheaval.
Buckinghamshire, an inland county offering geo-
graphical security yet proximity to London, was a
favorite refuge for numerous French émigrés who
fled the terrors of revolutionary violence. By 1792
French priests were settling in the county, and in
1796 Edmund Burke founded a school for young
aristocratic refugees at Penn, a few miles south of
Great Missenden. Lloyd may have visited the school,
met French priests in Great Missenden, or come into

8. See. W.T. Laprade, *England and the French Revolution, 1789-1797*
(Baltimore, 1909).

9. Edmund Burke, *The Works of Edmund Burke*, 2 vols. (1894), II
[Reflections on the Revolution in France], 305-7.

contact with French Catholics in some other way. Probably some *émigrés* visited the home of the Lloyds' landlord, Lord Dormer, himself a Roman Catholic. Certainly young Lloyd was impressed with the civility and integrity of those French Catholics, an impression which later contributed to his defense of Roman Catholicism before his pupils at Oxford and his peers in the House of Lords. "My lords," he reminisced in 1829, "much of my early life was spent in the company of Roman Catholics of the Gallican Church — of men, my lords, virtuous and religious."[10] Out of those youthful impressions were to flow profound consequences for the future political and ecclesiastical history of England.

In 1800 Lloyd, at 15 years of age, was sent to Eton. Like the other public schools, Eton had fallen on bad times academically. The Provost, Dr. Jonathan Davies, lived much of the time in London. While masters worked little and drank heavily, students gambled, fought, engaged in corporal punishments, played football and cricket, and poached pigs, fish and hare from the King's Little Park in Windsor. Little work was required beyond the memorization of some Greek and Latin poetry. Infrequent construing was perfunctory, and one could always find an old copy of the same exercise, repeated annually by indifferent teachers and preserved diligently by Etonians. In the early years of the nineteenth century an Eton pupil "probably knew somehow or other that 'two and two make four,' but

10. *Hansard's Parliamentary Debates,* new series, XXI (1829), 82. On the *émigrés,* see M. Weiner, *The French Exiles 1789-1815* (1960).

they might make three or five, as far as [the tutor] was concerned, without giving 'Henry's holy shade' the slightest annoyance." If one had the mind to do so, one could avoid work altogether.[11]

Yet Eton represented the best of places to establish pleasant friendships and useful connections. Lloyd's contemporaries were an impressive gathering of future earls, Lords-lieutenant, justices of the peace, members of Parliament, clerks in chancery, barristers and solicitors. Out of 127 members of his upper division of the Fifth Form in 1802, there were 29 future clergymen. Two were bishops-to-be: Lloyd (Oxford) and John Lonsdale (Lichfield). Of the 14 young men who would become military officers, four would be killed in the Napoleonic War, and another 14 were destined for posts in the colonies or India. Robert Marsham, a future Warden of Merton College, Oxford, was in Lloyd's class, as was a future Provost of Eton, E.C. Hawtrey. One member of the Fifth Form of 1802, destined to be a "Banker and Brewer," appears to be out of place among such a promising group of establishment leaders.[12]

Lloyd himself felt somewhat out of place. Whereas to the casual observer all Etonians appeared to be of the privileged aristocracy, there were, in fact, definite gradations of social rank within the school. Young Lloyd was among the group of social "inferiors," the collegers, who were supported by foundation scholarships because their fathers could not afford the high costs of tuition and board. In his

11. Christopher Hollis, *Eton. A History* (1960), pp. 176, 185-8; F.H. Doyle, *Reminiscences and Opinions, 1813-1885* (1886), p. 29-30.

12. H.E.C. Stapylton, *The Eton School Lists, from 1791 to 1850* (1854), pp. 38-40.

coarse cloth gown, "the peculiar badge and external form of being a Colleger," Lloyd was marked as a "Tug Mutton" by his superiors, the oppidans. The collegers were herded together in the notoriously drafty and noisy Long Chamber while the oppidans were allowed to live in the town, where they were treated as gentlemen in the tidy homes of dames or tutors. The collegers received shorter holidays than did the oppidans; upon leaving Eton they were denied the dubious honor of giving gifts of money or plate to the Headmaster, as was the custom with the oppidans.[13]

One of Lloyd's pupils at Oxford later conjectured that the colleger experience of inferior status at Eton marked Lloyd for life, making him edgy and unsure of himself.[14] The explanation is plausible. Yet several aspects of Lloyd's youth, all felt keenly at Eton, contributed to his sense of uneasiness. In addition to the tensions inherent in his attempt to break into an established aristocratic order, young Lloyd himself was short and somewhat fat, physical features hardly designed to make him an overly popular lad in a situation given more to frolic and games than to intellectual achievement. Most importantly, his older brother, in whom high paternal expectations had been centered, died at Eton in the very year of Charles' matriculation. Lacking the attention and natural confidence which usually come

13. [H.J.C. Blake], *Reminiscences of Eton* (Chichester, 1831), pp. 45, 70, 106; E.C. Mack, *Public Schools and British Opinion 1780 to 1860* (1938), p.78; Hollis, *Eton,* p.175.

14. G.R. Chinnery to Mary Chinnery, February 19, 1810, Ch. Ch. MS. xlix, fol. 64. Doubtless Lloyd was not the first Etonian to feel the effects of being a colleger; certainly he was not the last. Eric Blair (George Orwell) suffered similarly: Peter Stansky and William Abrahams, *The Unknown Orwell* (New York, 1972), pp. 89-90.

of being the first born son, Charles nevertheless after 1800 had transferred onto his own shoulders all the family's ambitions concerning the oldest male. His subsequent insatiable ambition and an aggressive, bluff pattern of social behavior served as covers for a deep-seated sense of inadequacy. He was thrust into a role for which he was psychologically ill-prepared.

No doubt Eton influenced Lloyd's move towards a political Toryism, a transition which came to fruition at Oxford. Eton having been a Tory stronghold since the Restoration of 1660, memoirs in the early nineteenth century abound with anecdotes concerning the school's connections with the royal court. Each year the birthday of the King was celebrated with a rowing contest, followed by a supper at which members of the royal family were usually present. King George III, with his colorful entourage, often passed through Eton on his way to stag-hunt between Slough and Langley Broom, and he held annual fetes for the boys of the upper forms. "Living as Etonians do under the immediate wing of Royalty," as one of Lloyd's contemporaries noted, "they have always, as a body of youth, been attached to their King and the Constitution of the land."[15] Apparently young Lloyd had little inclination to go against that Tory stream.

Upon finishing at Eton, he matriculated at Christ Church, Oxford, in February, 1803. Before the railway and the encroachment of industry, Oxford in the early nineteenth century was a sleepy little town whose inhabitants, just over 12,000, were intrinsically linked in service to the University. Fine

---

15. Blake, *Reminiscences of Eton*, p. 41. Blake matriculated at Eton in 1799, only one year before Lloyd.

spires and towers could be seen from afar. Few suburban dwellings obscured the view of open meadows and fields of grain adjoining the town. Magnificent elm trees lined the streets. As term began, coaches streamed into Oxford from all directions, filled with cloaked undergraduates and heaped high with trunks and baggage.[16]

With spires and towers reminiscent of a medieval past, an ecclesiastical atmosphere permeated the place. Oxford had long considered its primary purpose to be the "breeding of godly and learned divines." Only men in Anglican religious orders could hold most fellowships or professorships in the University. A fictitious "Spanish" visitor imagined himself back home in monastic, clerical Spain as he observed young and old men attired in dark garb "not unlike that of a secular priest." Even undergraduates were dressed in dark academic gowns, with gold tassels on caps distinguishing the sons of nobility.[17]

Lloyd found Oxford to be like Eton in the sense that most students were sons of the English aristocracy or status-seeking sons of highly successful merchants. Poorer students were invariably like himself, sons of clergymen. More than at any time in the past, Oxford in the early nineteenth century was an aristocratic body. For 200 years the number of students of plebeian origin (sons of husbandmen, craftsmen, artisans, and small shopkeepers) had been gradually declining. In the seventeenth and eighteenth centuries, young aristocrats and sons of

16. J. Meade Falkner, *A History of Oxfordshire* (1899), p. 315; William Tuckwell, *Reminiscences of Oxford* (1900), pp. 3-4.

17. Robert Southey, *Letters from England by Don Manuel Alvarez Espriella*, 2 vols. (1808), II, 2-3.

clergymen had squeezed the lower classes out of jobs in the church and educational institutions, leaving plebeians with little practical motivation for obtaining a university degree. Moreover, scholarships to Oxford colleges had been increasingly given to the privileged few, well-born or well-connected, at a time when the cost of education — for pre-university Latin training as well as for the University itself — was rising sharply. With financial as well as vocational practicalities having virtually excluded the poor, by 1803 Oxford students of non-clerical or non-aristocratic background numbered only four percent of the entire student body, compared to over 30 percent in 1703 and 40 percent in 1603.[18]

The Oxford which Charles Lloyd entered was a bastion of Tory influence as well as ecclesiastical and aristocratic exclusiveness. In the distant past the University had served as the court of the beleaguered Charles I, during the Puritan rebellion. For the first half of the eighteenth century, however, it stood in opposition to Whig governments and Hanoverian monarchs, finally to be drawn back into the orbit of Court and ministerial politics during the reign of George III. Faithfully mirroring the established order which was threatened by war and revolution throughout Europe in the age of Napoleon, the University regularly cast its weight in the constitutional struggles of the day. It was, as

18. Lawrence Stone, "The Size and Composition of the Oxford Student Body 1580-1910," in Lawrence Stone (ed.), *The University in Society*, 2 vols. (Princeton, 1974), I, 37-46. See especially the graph of the social status of matriculants, from 1580 to 1909 (p. 20). Although Lloyd's Oxford was notably aristocratic, the highest scale of the social spectrum (peers, baronets, and knights) were largely absent from the student body — for reasons vastly different from the plebeians (pp. 46-56).

W.R. Ward has suggested, "a privileged oracle of the *ancien régime*."[19] Yet never had the University's reputation as an educational institution been so low. In the second half of the eighteenth century, critics from within and without portrayed tutors, heads of houses, and professors as being sunk in apathy, sloth, drunkenness, and petty politics. Little attention seemed to be given to good teaching and scholarship was deemed to be virtually beside the point of university life. According to critics, undergraduates saw Oxford merely as an extension of the leisurely, indulgent life of the clergy or country gentlemen. Generously financed by their fathers and academically unchallenged by their tutors, young men apparently turned to the delights of hunting and shooting, tandem-driving, boating, hack-riding, smoking, drinking, whoring, betting and card-playing, rather than to the rigors of lectures and libraries.

The most severe critic of Oxford's malaise was Edward Gibbon, who insisted that he endured fourteen months of "the most idle and unprofitable" period of his life at Magdalen College in 1752-53. Perceiving the spirit of the University to be "narrow, lazy, and oppressive," Gibbon discovered that Oxford professors had "given up altogether even the pretense of teaching." The fellows of Magdalen, "decent easy men, who supinely enjoyed the gifts of the founder," were a lethargic lot. Bigoted and indif-

---

19. Ward, *Victorian Oxford*, p. xiii. For the reconciliation of Court and University in the 1770's, see Ward's *Georgian Oxford: University Politics in the Eighteenth Century* (Oxford, 1958), pp. 239-79. Compare Cambridge, more consistently Whig, in D.A. Winstanley, *The University of Cambridge in the 18th Century* (Cambridge, 1958).

ferent to the world at large, they filled their days
with "the chapel and the hall, the coffee-house and
the common room, till they retired, weary and well
satisfied, to a long slumber." Intellectual issues held
little attraction: "From the toil of reading, or thinking, or writing, they had absolved their conscience....
Their conversation stagnated in a round of college
business, Tory politics, personal anecdotes, and
private scandal." Such tutors could provide neither
inspiration nor discipline for even the most eager
undergraduate. His own tutor remaining a virtual
stranger, Gibbon studied only three or four Latin
plays during his fourteen months at Oxford. Not until he left the University did his taste for books revive.[20]

Although Gibbon cannot be dismissed lightly,
there is little doubt that his experience was unusually bad, and that his account was overly biased.
Unabashedly anti-clerical by the time he wrote his
autobiography, he could hardly sympathize with an
institution whose purpose and tone were ecclesiastical. More importantly, he was a Gentleman
Commoner at Oxford, a category of undergraduates
who, not expected even to take a degree, were
seldom in residence for the entire term and were
often arrogant towards their tutors whom they considered their social inferiors. Certainly one should
not generalize on the state of the University solely
from Gibbon's particular case at a single college, no
matter how bad it was.

But Gibbon was not, in fact, a lone critic. Whereas
he censored the lethargy of college life, others
harshly indicted the fiasco of an oral exercise, loosely

20. Edward Gibbon, *The Autobiography of Edward Gibbon* (1920), pp. 40-47.

referred to as an "examination," prior to the taking
of a degree. Topics of disputation were handed
down from generation to generation. Each college
determined its own procedure, with no standards
established by the University at large. At St.
John's College in the 1770's two undergraduates entered a
large, dusty room, sat in small desks across from
each other, and whiled away two hours writing a few
verses and reading some novel or newspapers.[21]
From University College John Scott (later Lord
Chancellor Eldon) received his B.A. in 1770 on the
strength of satisfactory answers to two questions: (1)
What is the Hebrew for the place of a skull? and (2)
Who founded University College? His answers —
Golgotha and King Alfred — were deemed sufficient
evidence of his academic achievement. "Very well,
sir," said his examiner, "you are competent for your
degree." Well could Lord Eldon note much later
that "an examination for a degree at Oxford was a
farce in my time."[22] In 1774 young Henry Addington (later First Viscount Sidmouth), an undergraduate about to take his degree at Brasenose,
assured his father that he "was under no anxiety on
account of the disputations." Addington was
"credibly informed" by his contemporaries that the
examinations were "mere farces."[23]

21. Vicesimus Knox, *On Some Parts of the Discipline in our English
    Universities* (1778), cited in C.E. Mallet, *A History of the University of
    Oxford*, 3 vols. (1927), III, 163-64.

22. Horace Twiss, *The Public and Private Life of Lord Chancellor Eldon, with
    Selections from his Correspondence*. 3 vols. (1844), I, 57. A Victorian
    memoirist, G.V. Cox, looked on this anecdote as a mere "post pran-
    dium joke": *Recollections of Oxford* (1868), p. 34, n. 1.

23. George Pellew, *The Life and Correspondence of the Right Honourable
    Henry Addington, First Viscount Sidmouth*, 3 vols. (1847), I, 20.

When graduates wrote their memoirs in the nineteenth century, they universally lamented the low
level of Oxford life before 1800. In an attempt to
balance the picture, recent historians such as Steven
Watson argue that "the decadence of the universities
has perhaps been exaggerated by nineteenth-century reformers," and that "everything depended upon the character of particular tutors and
pupils" as "the drunken don and his studious
colleague lived side by side within the tolerant
academic shades."[24] But Victorian judgment cannot
be dismissed as the mere retroactive negativism of
men overly impressed with the progress that they
observed in their mature years. The Victorians were
not wrong in what they saw, but simply unhelpful in
fostering historical understanding; their self-
righteous condemnations precluded their probing
for the causes of what they described.[25]

Present research is geared to replacing denuncia-
tions with understanding. W.R. Ward, for example,
suggests that the onerous burden of manning the
political and ecclesiastical ramparts of society distracted Georgian Oxford from giving serious attention to teaching and research.[26] Another line of
explanation is offered in the recent work of
Lawrence Stone, who examines Oxford within the
social shifts of wealth and value-structures,
technological changes (such as communications and
transportation), and the relationship of the supply of
university-trained men to the demand for them.

24. Watson, *The Reign of George III*, p. 40.
25. See Arthur Engel, "Emerging Concepts of the Academic Profession
    at Oxford 1800-1854," in Stone (ed.), *The University in Society*, I, 308.
26. Ward, *Victorian Oxford*, xiv-xv.

Stone documents Oxford's "numerical depression" in the eighteenth century, revealing that from 1750 to 1800 the University attracted the fewest students at any time in its modern history. In such times of numerical depression, he argues, "the university tended to become introverted, and withdrawn from the center of affairs, cut off from the vital flow of young men and from the interchange of ideas and values they brought with them." Dons narrowed their scope of interest, and the bracing air of the Enlightenment largely passed them by; the University's curriculum became frozen in its old classical molds.[27]

In her recent James Bryce Memorial Lecture, Dame Lucy Sutherland set out "to consider how far the general [negative] opinion of eighteenth-century Oxford was justified." She rightly insisted that the University's malaise has been "grossly exaggerated." Eighteenth-century Oxford was shackled with the outmoded Laudian code of Statutes of 1636 which prescribed a confining curriculum and an inadequate degree structure, but "on the credit side" many undergraduates, ignored by their tutors, "found things out for themselves" from free-lance teachers, in intimate study groups, and through systematic courses of lectures offered outside the University curriculum. Yet even the most eager revisionist cannot erase the fact that Oxford lacked inspiration, vitality, and intellectual distinction. Despite all the "opportunities of books and learned

27. Stone, "The Size and Composition of the Oxford Student Body 1580-1910," in *The University in Society*, I, p.5. See the graph of estimated freshman admissions (p. 6): the number of matriculants dropped from 500 in 1620 to a low of less than 200 in the 1750's; by 1800 annual freshman admissions were still less than 250.

men," as Dr. Johnson noted in 1768, the members of Oxford were "for a season ... unmindful of their duty."[28]

Even in its most somnolent days, however, the university was not bereft of internal criticism and demands for reform. Cambridge introduced university examinations for honors degrees in the 1770's, and as early as 1773 a similar plan was formally proposed to Oxford, commended by the Vice-Chancellor, and discussed by the heads of houses and proctors. Specific times and procedures were outlined for a fully public examination, all designed to make it "a formidable ordeal." But nothing came of the proposal; lethargy and vested interests won the day.[29]

Still, the case for reform was not dismissed. Having realigned itself with the Court and establishment politics, the University could scarcely remain indifferent to the reforming impetus provided by the government of William Pitt the younger. Moreover, Oxford's ineptitude was held up to public scorn in pamphlets and memoirs throughout the last quarter of the eighteenth century, culminating in Gibbon's

28. Dame Lucy Sutherland, *The University of Oxford in the Eighteenth Century; a Reconsideration* (Oxford, 1973).

29. Christopher Wordsworth, *Scholae Academiae: Some Account of the Studies at the English Universities in the Eighteenth Century* (Cambridge, 1910), p. 215-6.

vicious assault in 1796. First published in his *Miscellaneous Works*, Gibbon's critique created no small sensation, coming as it did from the pen of one of England's most illustrious men of letters, the author of the monumental *Decline and Fall of the Roman Empire*. Confronted with his public, much-debated insistence on governmental intervention in academic areas historically protected by chartered liberties, even the most addled of Oxford's "idle monks" were aroused to the need to set their own house in order.[30]

Gibbon himself recognized some points of excellence. A number of professors, especially in various fields of science, were delivering regular learned lectures which were attracting large audiences of undergraduates. Improvements were taking place at several colleges, particularly at Christ Church where "a more regular discipline" had been introduced, and learning had been made "a duty, a pleasure, and even a fashion."[31]

In 1783 Cyril Jackson, an energetic, domineering man who detested mediocrity as much as insubordination, became the Dean of Christ Church. Under his direction Christ Church asserted itself not only as a political force but also as the leader of Oxford's academic renewal. Although Jackson tended to view the University solely in terms of the interests of his own college, he well knew that Christ Church would remain a vulnerable station in the wilderness unless the University as a whole were revived. Thus is 1800 he joined forces with John Eveleigh, Provost of Oriel, and John Parsons, Master of Balliol, to establish a new system of University examinations.

30. Ward, *Victorian Oxford*, p. 6.

31. Gibbon, *Autobiography*, p. 59.

Specific details concerning the motives and negotiations behind the new examinations are shrouded in obscurity. Recently Sheldon Rothblatt has reasoned convincingly that few traces of a "meritocratic ideal" can be detected in the deliberations, that Oxford dons were concerned primarily with creating a means of discipline for unruly undergraduates whose sense of unfettered independence had flowered under liberal Enlightenment theories of child-rearing and French revolutionary ideas.[32] Whatever the original impetus, one can be sure that Cyril Jackson and his colleagues were acting as self-interested rationalists rather than liberal reformists, and that the motive of control was never far in the background.

The examination statute of 1800 created an honors degree. The responsibility for honors examinations was taken out of the hands of individual colleges, and the exercise was to be fully public "with as many members of the university as possible" in attendance. Six examiners were to be elected each year, and at least three were to be present at each examination. Candidates were still tested orally *(viva voce)* on the traditional subjects of grammar, rhetoric, logic, moral philosphy and physics — and on a new subject,"the Elements of Religion, and the Doctrinal Articles of 1562." An honors degree would be awarded those candidates who distinguished themselves in the examinations, but an undergraduate could choose simply to take his B.A.

32. Sheldon Rothblatt, "The Student Sub-culture and the Examination System in Early 19th Century Oxbridge" in Stone (ed.), *The University in Society*, I, 280-88.

on the basis of traditional college examinations.[33]
By the time of Charles Lloyd's arrival in 1803, the
new examinations were considered "so serious and
severe" by Oxford undergraduates that some were
speaking "with envy of the happy days of their predecessors."[34] No doubt many young aristocrats
looked upon such a hurdle, in which they were put
on the spot and criticized publicly, as beneath their
dignity. Others simply did not believe that an honors
degree was worth the strenuous effort of preparation. From 1802 to 1806 only 13 candidates presented themselves for honors degrees.[35] But to young
men of ambition, such as Lloyd, the new examinations were welcome because they provided "distinctions to Persons approving themselves to the Examiners in a superior way to the rest."[36] Merit,
rather than mere birth or connections, was forging
its way, haltingly, at Oxford. Charles Lloyd was
fortunate in the timing of his matriculation.

He was also fortunate to be at Christ Church. In
an era when one's academic as well as social life centered far more in the college than in the University
at large, it was of supreme advantage to be a
member of the largest, wealthiest, and most prestigious of all the colleges at Oxford. Because of its
size (which made it less susceptible to the doleful effects of the "numerical depression" of matriculants
in the eighteenth century), unique constitution, and

33. For details of the new examination statute, see Mallet, *History of Oxford*, III, 167-69, and Ward, *Victorian Oxford*, pp. 12-16.

34. Southey, *Letters from Oxford*, II, 19.

35. Wordsworth, *Scholae Academiae*, p. 222.

36. Mallet, *History of Oxford*, III, 168.

exceptional heads, Christ Church had never suc-
cumbed to the apathy of which Gibbon complained.
Unlike most of the University, it had since 1714
been closely associated with the Hanoverian court,
consciously striving to produce the future leaders of
Church and State. As it served as a nursery for "the
Establishment," Christ Church was simply being true
to its past. From its beginnings, it was both a college
and a cathedral, representing a rare blending of
political, educational, and ecclesiastical interests. According to its foundation charter, granted by Henry
VIII in 1546, a Dean and eight Canons (the
Chapter) were designated as the legal corporation,
the Governing Body, to be appointed by the Crown
rather than by election or episcopal appointment; in
the early seventeenth century the University's
Regius Chairs of Divinity and Hebrew were attached
to two of the Canonries.[37]

Christ Church was unique among Oxford colleges
in that it had no statutes defining its constitution and
government. The Dean and Chapter governed
largely by customs and precedents which by the early nineteenth century had assumed the authority of
statutes which could still be circumvented when
necessary. Given this flexibility, the Dean and
Chapter exercised enormous authority. They administered the vast estates owned by the college,
controlled the internal economy, presented clerics to
the ninety college livings, and appointed under-

---

37. For the constitution and governance of "the old Christ Church"
(before mid-nineteenth century reforms), see E.G.W. Bill and J.F.A.
Mason, *Christ Church and Reform 1850-1867* (Oxford, 1970), pp.
1-23.

graduates to Studentships. The Dean was the dominant figure. Unlike most of the Canons, he was always resident during the term, admitting undergraduates, appointing tutors and Servitors (poorer undergraduates who made their way by performing menial tasks), and making appointments to Exhibitions.

The Dean was assisted in his administrative and academic responsibilities by two executive officers drawn from the body of Students, the Senior and Junior Censors. Although not members of the Governing Body, the Censors were responsible for tuition and discipline in the college. A Censorship was a most important, dignified, and lucrative position which often led to a Canonry and occasionally even to one of the Canonries attached to the Regius Chair of Divinity or Hebrew. The path of Charles Lloyd's own success, in fact, lay in the progression from Censor to the Regius Professorship of Divinity.

At his matriculation in 1803, of course, Lloyd's success lay far in the distant future. First he had to become a Student, a position with specific meaning unique to Christ Church. Not all undergraduates were designated as Students. One Christ Church man defined a Studentship as an honor "peculiar to Christ Church; something between a scholarship and a fellowship at other colleges,"[38] but such comparisons conceal as much as they reveal. Whereas fellows in Oxford colleges were graduates, of the 101 Students at Christ Church, almost half were undergraduates. Unlike fellows, Students were not al-

---

38. Charles Wordsworth, *Annals of My Early Life,* 1806-1846 (1891), p. 43.

lowed to participate in the governance of the college,
nor were their stipends large enough to support
them without some other means of income. Many
fellowships and most scholarships were reserved for
the kin of the founders or benefactors, or for a
particular locality; very few Studentships were
closed. Three were reserved each year for boys
from Westminster School and one was appointed
by the descendant of an early benefactor. The remaining Studentships were open to all members of
Christ Church, except Servitors.

As Studentships became vacant, appointments
were made by the Dean and Chapter in rotation,
with the Dean having two turns and each Canon
one. Although liable to the abuse of unprincipled
patronage, this system allowed the Dean and Canons
to keep their eyes open for young men of character,
ability, and industry, and to base their selections on
need as well as merit. Studentships entailed no pro-
bationary year, as did most fellowships. Thus the
Dean and Chapter demanded residence prior to
"election" (appointment). It was an arrangement
peculiarly suited to a young man such as Lloyd, who
apparently possessed the knack of making a favor-
able impression on his superiors.

Yet another Christ Church tradition weighed
heavily against Lloyd's prospects. Christ Church had
long exercised a pronounced bias in favor of men
from Westminster School, not Eton. Westminster
School dominated the Student ranks as thoroughly
as it did the entire body of undergraduates. Most
tutors and Censors, as well as Deans (all three during Lloyd's entire association with Christ Church,
1803-1829), were from Westminster School. Lloyd's
tenure at Eton, while not necessarily a mark against

him, was not a factor working in his favor at Christ
Church.

Much to his advantage, however, was the
character of his Dean, Cyril Jackson. Dean Jackson
was already a legend in his own time. Eccentric and
opinionated, arrogant and persuasive, he ruled
Christ Church with an iron hand. Various Christ
Church men referred to him as "our Great King,"
"the supreme Potentate," and the head of "an
absolute monarchy of the most ultra-oriental
character."[39] He was not without his critics. One Oxford man referred to him as "something of a moun-
tebank," and another more harshly dismissed him as
"an 'inspired swine,' who preached exceeding dry
sermons with a prodigious degree of snuffling."[40]
But critics and admirers agreed on one thing: Cyril
Jackson was a force to be reckoned with. Because of
his power of personality as well as his prestigious
position, he could not easily be ignored.

Nor did Jackson himself ignore undergraduates
under his charge. He was a most ardent exponent of
the virtues of hard work. To his undergraduates he

39. Alexander Allardyce (ed.), *Letters from and to Charles Kirkpatrick
    Sharpe,* 2 vols. (1888), I, 140; G.R. Chinnery to Mary Chinnery,
    January 25, 1808, Ch. Ch. MS. xlii, fol. 46; [Amelia Heber], *The Life
    of Reginald Heber,* 2 vols. (1830), I, 499.

40. [J.W. Ward], *Letters of the Earl of Dudley to the Bishop of Llandaff,*
    (1840), p. 192-3; Allardyce, *Sharpe,* I, 11.

insisted, as he later wrote to Robert Peel, that one
should work "like a tiger, or like a dragon, if
dragons work more and harder than tigers." While
being temperate and getting enough physical exercise, a young Christ Church man was instructed
from the outset to practice an "aversion to mere
lounge" in order to have "abundant time both for
hard work and company." Though the cultivation of
good connections was indispensable to one's future
success and happiness, good company to the ex-
clusion of intellectual vigor was anathema. According to Jackson, hard work was not beneath the
dignity of a gentleman, even a Christ Church
gentleman.[41] Certainly it was not beneath the dignity
of an able youth from Buckinghamshire whose future
prospects depended on academic achievement
rather than birth.

In style as well as perspective, Lloyd was greatly
influenced by Jackson. At the most obvious level, he
picked up the Dean's eccentric mannerisms. In that
age when "the academic eccentrics, of which there
were legion, were grotesque in their eccentricity, "[42]
Cyril Jackson shaped the public style of an entire
generation of Christ Church men. A dark, bulky
coat, the cocking of the head to the side, the tilting
of the academic hat on the bridge of the nose, and

41. C. S. Parker, *Sir Robert Peel from his Private Papers*, 3 vols.
(1891-9), I, 29. In 1809 Jackson wrote to Sir Charles Bagot, a Christ
Church graduate who was being relieved of his governmental office:
"Now to talk as if we were still at Ch. Ch. — . . . Use the time of retirement well, read and labour hard. You must now be fully
enabled to judge what those points are, on which you feel that you
either want information totally or that more would be of service to
you. Pursue those points *unremittingly*." J.F. Bagot, *George Canning
and his Friends*, 2 vols. (1909), I, 320.

42. Newsome, *The Parting of Friends*, p. 64.

the taking of snuff all became symbols of a select group made in the image of the old Dean. Yet Lloyd took on more of Jackson's style than those mere touches of peculiar appearance. From the Dean he also learned the art of the sharp question, the abrupt, well-turned retort, and the air of cynical aloofness.

Moreover, he imbibed the Dean's perspective concerning the exclusive superiority of Christ Church. Chauvinistic to the core, Jackson carried the idea of "Christ Church pride" to its extreme. He refused to have his undergraduates taught by private tutors in other colleges, required them to use the services only of physicians in Oxford who were Christ Church men, and discouraged them from making too many friends outside the college.[43] Though ill-reasoned, his rationalization was simple: "I say nothing in disparagement of other colleges: no doubt there are clever men to be found in them: but as Christ-Church is the largest college in the university, there must be more men of sense in this college than in any other, by the rule of proportion simply." This fragile explanation left him open for a reminder from one clever gentleman commoner that there must be "more fools, too, by the same rule."[44] Still, the Dean never wavered from his insistence that Christ Church was not only bigger and better than the other Oxford colleges, but sufficient in and of itself for social intercourse as well as academic pursuits. This perspective largely explains why

43. G.R. Chinnery to Mary Chinnery, March 4, 1808, Ch. Ch. MS. xliii, fols. 23-24; G.V. Cox, *Recollections of Oxford* (1868), p. 163.

44. [H.D. Beste], *Personal and Literary Memorials* (1829), pp. 103-4. But to anyone who questioned one of his orders, Jackson replied simply, "The dean of Christ-Church speaks but once." (p. 101).

Lloyd's closest friends were usually Christ Church
men. Nor can his later jibes at other colleges be fully
appreciated apart from his instinctive attachment to
what Edward Copleston once called the "little pla-
toon" of Christ Church society.[45]

Although Cyril Jackson encouraged a narrowness
in social contact, he fostered a broad vision of the
duties pressing upon a Christ Church man. Christ
Church was exclusive and proud, but not monastic.
Jackson never considered his own influence to be
confined within the cloistered walls. He was one of
the leaders in the realignment of the University with
the royal court in the late-eighteenth century; in
1803, the year of Lloyd's matriculation, he was busily
manipulating affairs to bring Pitt back in at the head
of a new government.[46] In the apt words of an historian of the college, Jackson's influence penetrated
"far beyond the walls of Christ Church to English
society at large, where — in the greater world of action — statesmen, divines, and men of letters
showed the results of his wise government."[47] He
urged his abler students to think in similarly large
terms. The wide range of Lloyd's subsequent activities — educational, ecclesiastical, and political —
mirrored the versatility inculcated by Dean Jackson.

Jackson was not, of course, Lloyd's tutor; Edmund
Goodenough played that role.[48] But the Dean was
never far in the background. When an undergraduate first arrived at Christ Church, he had an
audience with Jackson, and at the beginning of each

45. Ward, *Letters of Dudley to Llandaff*, p. 192.
46. Ward, *Victorian Oxford*, p. 10.
47. H.L. Thompson, *Christ Church* (1900), p. 175.
48. Christ Church Caution Book, 1743 to 1804.

term he was called upon to report his holiday activities and the prospectus of work to be done. Assuming the importance of the classics, Jackson was especially eager to encourage the study of mathematics. Although he was like most of his English contemporaries in being a century behind time in his mathematical understanding — clinging to unrevised, out-moded Newtonian fluxions while disdaining the differential method of analysis pioneered by continental mathematicians in the eighteenth century[49] — he nevertheless had a name for being a clever mathematician in his own right. Occasionally he quizzed undergraduates or delivered incredibly complex orations to them on the subject of mathematics.[50] Apparently Lloyd profited from this expertise, as he himself was soon to be considered the best mathematics tutor in the University.

More importantly, Dean Jackson possessed a keen eye for talent. It was rightly said that he "made it his especial duty to know the members of his House, to watch their several intimacies and habits, and to scan their feelings and their excellencies."[51] Upon spotting a particularly bright man, the Dean took pride in nominating him to a Studentship. In December, 1804, Lloyd was named the "Dean's Student," probably not only because of his obvious ability in mathematics, but also as a testimony to his eager willingness to work hard. The Dean's nomination

49. See C.B. Boyer, *The History of the Calculus and its Conceptual Development* (New York, 1949), p. 302.

50. G.R. Chinnery to Mary Chinnery, January 27, 1808, Ch. Ch. MS. xlii, fol. 58.

51. *Gentleman's Magazine* XCIX (1829), 561; cf. E.H. Barker, *Parriana; or Notices of the Rev. Samuel Parr,* 2 vols. (1828), I, 421-3.

was shown to be fully justified in 1806, when Lloyd emerged from his three-day examination with highest honors: *"Examinatoribus publicis se maxime commendavit."* There was no question that he deserved his Bachelor's degree: *"Admissus ad Gradum A.B. Simpliciter."*[52] Nor was there any question, on the part of those who knew him well, that he was destined for greater things.

---

52. Christ Church Collections Book, 1803-1806, p. 321.

II A TUTOR HIGHLY ESTEEMED

SHORTLY AFTER HE RECEIVED his degree in 1806, Lloyd went to Scotland to serve as a private tutor to the children of Lord Elgin at Dunfermline. Unfortunately no evidence has survived to shed light on the year, but certainly Lloyd did not remain long at the post. In 1807 he was summoned back to Christ Church by Dean Jackson, to serve as a tutor and lecturer in mathematics.[1] While Napoleon turned against Russia and Britain struggled against the

---

1. *Gentleman's Magazine,* XCIX (1829), 561. I am grateful to the present Lord Elgin for kindly investigating old family manuscript letters and writing to me on February 25 and October 28, 1969. A let-

Continental embargo, Charles Lloyd, at 23 years of age, was launching his academic career. He was to remain a tutor of Christ Church for the next twelve years, holding in turn the subordinate posts, then assigned to those performing the tutorial work of the House, of Greek Reader and Rhetoric Reader.[2]

One of his first assignments at Christ Church was the supervision of young Robert Peel's studies. Peel, having selected his activities and companions — as his official biographer put it — "less with a view to intellectual intercourse than to social enjoyment," had expended little intellectual energy during his first two years as an undergraduate. By the time Lloyd returned to Christ Church, however, Peel was ready to settle down to work in preparation for the examination facing him at the end of Michaelmas Term, 1808. And work they did. Young Peel studied eighteen hours each day for his last two or three terms, and Lloyd was at his side much of the time, prodding him on, overseeing his progress and offering encouragement. Years later Lloyd remarked that Peel "always did what he was bid and never minded work," which is to say that as Lloyd was a tutor in the style of Cyril Jackson, Peel was a man cut from a similar mold.[3]

On a superficial level the two men were vastly different. Peel, from Harrow, was tall, well-dressed and handsome; Lloyd, an Etonian, was short, heavy-set,

---

ter of the earlier Lady Elgin, dated, January 1, 1806, indicates that the children's tutor, a Mr. Macfarlane, was leaving; but no reference to Lloyd can be found. Lord Elgin was a political prisoner in France at the time.

2. Christ Church Chapter Minute Book, 1802-21, p. 197.

3. Parker, *Peel*, I, 19-21; Arthur Aspinall (ed.), *Three Nineteenth Century Diaries* (1952), p. 119.

and slovenly. Whereas Peel was casual and confident, Lloyd was fastidious, always thorough but
often laborious, anxiously given to details that were
sometimes beside the point. Yet they had much in
common. With only four years separating them in
age, both men enjoyed the give-and-take of intellectual banter; both loved to ride and hunt (Lloyd, sur-
prisingly, being a better rider than Peel), and both
were firm believers in Cyril Jackson's principle of
hard work. Each, in fact, supplied those qualities
lacking in the other. For Peel, Lloyd represented an
attention to detail, a fussy but necessary willingness
to look ahead, manipulate, and barge through doors
half-open. Peel, on the other hand, emitted an easy
superiority, an unforced, almost indifferent acceptance of the real, unadorned situation; an ability to
go with the tide, and in so doing to catch it at its
flood. These differences, mostly unspoken, were re-
cognised and accepted. "There existed between us,"
Peel wrote much later, "the most cordial attachment, and the habits of perfectly unreserved intercourse formed at college were continued without
the slightest interruption until. . .[Lloyd's death]
deprived me of a beloved and faithful friend."[4]

Both men were ambitious — Lloyd as an academic
and ecclesiastic, Peel as a politician. If Lloyd's origins
were relatively humble, Peel himself was something
of a newcomer to the status of gentleman commoner. His paternal grandfather started as a
yeoman farmer in Lancashire, and his father began
as a worker in a cotton mill, rose to the position of
clerk, succeeded in trade, and became a large land-
owner and member of Parliament. "Bob, you dog,"

4. Robert Peel, *Memoirs of the Right Honourable Sir Robert Peel,* ed. Earl
   Stanhope and Edward Cardwell (1857), I, 64.

young Peel had heard his father say only half in jest, "if you are not prime minister some day, I'll disinherit you."[5] At Christ Church Peel and Lloyd talked often and freely about their respective plans, hopes and anxieties concerning the future.

Personally attracted to each other as they were, their mutual ambitions lay at the center of their collaboration at Christ Church. With Peel universally "reckoned by far the cleverest man in Christ Church,"[6] Lloyd envisaged resounding success in the schools, and future greatness — and possibly helpfulness in terms of patronage — in the political sphere. Peel, on the other hand, saw in Lloyd a tutor who could get him through the examinations at the top of the heap; and one who, more importantly, formed a link with old Dean Jackson and his vast network of political connections. Even the tutorials were occasionally slanted to Peel's political interests. Just before the summer vacation of 1807, pupil and tutor discussed John Locke's praise of William Chillingworth's *Religion of Protestants a Safe Way of Salvation* (1638). Upon being told that Chillingworth was "a most powerful reasoner," Peel read the book during the summer and was examined orally on it when he returned to Christ Church in the autumn.[7]

5. Samuel Rogers, *Recollections of Samuel Rogers,* ed. "A.D." (1856), p. 250. According to one report, Lloyd himself once told Peel that his dignified composure made him suited for the House of Lords, provoking Peel to reply sharply that he wanted, instead, "to guide the destinies of this great Empire" and could do so only by carrying the people with him in the House of Commons: A.H.D. Acland (ed.), *Memoir and Letters of the Right Honourable Sir Thomas Dyke Acland* (1902), p. 130.

6. G.R. Chinnery to Mary Chinnery, February 14, 1808, Ch. Ch. MS. xlii, fol. 90.

7. Aspinall, *Three Diaries,* p. 119.

Never very interested in theology, he was certainly intent on developing the traits of a "powerful reasoner."

Peel's public examination on November 19, 1808, was one of those grand events which evoked awe and admiration from his contemporaries — "the most splendid thing they had ever heard." In a large room packed with undergraduates and dons, Lloyd proudly watched and listened as Peel responded adeptly to questions in ethics, logic, classics, mathematics, and divinity. His Latin and Greek constructions were perfect. He displayed himself "so completely master of every single thing in which he was examined" that his examiners cut short the exercise and expressed their hope that his example would be followed by others.[8] In fact, for years afterwards the performance was remembered in Oxford circles as a model of excellence.[9]

Although there was no doubt of Peel's innate brilliance, Lloyd's tutorials were of no small significance in the achievement of a Double-First degree. Their relationship, crowned with this initial success, was destined to be deepened and enlarged in the forthcoming years. Following his examinations, Peel stayed on at Christ Church until mid-December, then returned for a final term of study early in 1809. In April, 1809, he took a parliamentary seat for Cashel, a corrupt Irish borough. Shortly thereafter he wrote to Lloyd, expressing a desire to continue their friendship beyond the quadrangles

8. G.R. Chinnery to Mary Chinnery, November 20, 1808, Ch. Ch. MS. xlv, fol. 69. For the most familiar account of Peel's performance in the examination, see Parker, *Peel*, I, 22-23.

9. See J.T. Coleridge, *A Memoir of the Rev. John Keble* (Oxford and London, 1880), p. 47.

of Christ Church, "except," he added, "as regards conic sections and matters of that kind."[10]

Himself immersed in matters concerning conic sections, Greek verbs, and Latin authors, Lloyd for the time being was too busy with academic affairs to pursue further correspondence with Peel. He had reason to be concerned with several recent revisions of the examination statute of 1800. In 1807 Oxford's traditional classicists arranged for the examination in mathematics and physics to be separated from the classics and made optional, with classics being the only requirement. Mathematics and physics were thereby placed at a distinct disadvantage; other sciences, omitted altogether from the examination schedule, languished. Classes in chemistry, botany, mineralogy, and anatomy quickly dwindled, not to be revived for several decades at Oxford. Thus a narrowly classical curriculum was further narrowed.[11]

This triumph of the classicists did not go unchallenged. For many years Edward Tatham, the Rector of Lincoln College, railed against the overwhelming dominance of Aristotelian studies in the University. Another Oxford man complained that at Oxford the mind quickly lost "its plastic quality" as a result of the preponderance of classicism: "The place abounds in sense, learning and worth; but the power of giving a fair consideration to any thing that is, or appears, new, is precisely what it wants."[12] In 1808 and 1809 the prestigious Whig journal, *The Edinburgh Review,* levelled three successive attacks

10. Norman Gash, *Mr. Secretary Peel: The Life of Sir Robert Peel to 1830* (1961), p. 56.

11. See Ward, *Victorian Oxford,* pp. 14-16.

12. Ward, *Letters of Dudley to Llandaff,* p. 7, 8.

against "the dictates of Aristotle" being still "listened to as infallible decrees" to the detriment of mathematics, science, and modern languages. The core of the *Edinburgh's* complaint was "not that classical knowledge is not a good, but that it is the only good... [and] that we are making only one article, when we ought to be making many."[13] Charles Lloyd, more interested in mathematics than the classics, probably agreed with the main thrust of these criticisms.

What Lloyd's generation lacked in breadth, however, it gained in depth. As the standard, public examinations required Oxford undergraduates to take seriously their studies *in literis humanioribus,* the revised system had an even more dramatic effect on Oxford tutors and professors. Lectures became valuable for reasons other than their intrinsic worth. For the first time, standards were provided whereby the effectiveness of teaching could be measured. Success in the examinations came to be a matter of personal satisfaction and public prestige not only for the pupil, but for his tutor as well.

As a favorite disciple of Dean Jackson, Lloyd was assigned several private pupils whose performances in the examinations would inevitably reflect upon his own commitment and ability. The correspondence of one of those pupils, G.R. Chinnery, provides considerable insight into Lloyd's character as well as his teaching techniques. Young Chinnery wrote home to his parents almost every day from his matriculation in January, 1808, until his examinations in November, 1811. His sketch of his academic and social life within the University at large is interesting, but even more significant is his depiction of his rela-

13. See Ward, *Victorian Oxford,* pp. 17-19.

tionship with Lloyd, a portrayal that is all the more
valuable because it conveyed the impression Lloyd
made on an undergraduate. Nor was the impression
slight.

In an initial interview, Dean Jackson discovered
that young Chinnery had several deficiencies in his
education — at the hands of private tutors at Tun-
bridge Wells — prior to coming to Oxford. According to the Dean, Chinnery needed a private tutor at
Christ Church who would "retravel over the ground"
which earlier tutors had covered and proceed to "fill
up every little chink." At first, Jackson thought W.
J. Law the best man for the task; upon further
reflection, he selected Lloyd.[14].

After their first meeting on February 12, 1808,
Chinnery wrote to his mother that Lloyd appeared
to be "a very pleasant man, extremely good natured
& lively." The arrangement promised to be productive. At their first tutorial Lloyd began filling the
"chinks" in Chinnery's education. Actually, by Oxford standards there was a yawning gap to be filled.
Chinnery had never read Homer, an unpardonable
omission. Lloyd advised that an *Index Homericus* be
used beside a lexicon, in order to ascertain the
various usages, or sense, of each word in Homer.
This rather pedantic approach struck the eager
Chinnery as "an excellent plan; it takes scarcely any
time, and will undoubtedly make me acquainted
with an immense number of words." Responsive to
Lloyd's suggestion that he should concentrate solely

---

14. G.R. Chinnery to Mary Chinnery, January 15, 1808, Ch. Ch. MS.
xlii, fol. 5; February 10, 1808, xlii, fol. 77. All subsequent citations
from the Chinnery Correspondence are letters from son to mother,
unless otherwise indicated.

on Greek for the first term, Chinnery was "very much satisfied" with his new tutor.[15]

Like other tutors, Lloyd did not limit himself to one subject. Although it was misleading as well as melodramatic to suggest that scholarship in early-nineteenth century Oxford was "not technical but monumental,"[16] it was true that tutors were men of general rather than specialized interests. Lloyd supervised the study of Greek and Latin languages and literature, logic, ethics, history, religion, and all aspects of mathematics. Though he was a future Regius Professor of Divinity, the subject which he taught least was religion.[17]

His weakest subject was logic. Once he directed Chinnery to translate a number of syllogisms from Latin into English, then to memorize all the demonstrations by heart. Either Lloyd had no real grasp of the principles of logic or he was unable to communicate his knowledge to his pupil. Chinnery soon became thoroughly confused. He could not understand the public lectures in logic, and Lloyd could not shed any light on the subject. In exasperation Chinnery wrote his parents that logic was so impossibly difficult that "mechanics *recreate* the mind after logic." It took him several months to discover that his problem might lie in his tutor's limitations as much as in the intricacies of the subject itself. Finally he went to another tutor for help. "I find that Lloyd is not of the least use to me in logic," he wrote home with a sigh of relief, "for he confesses that he knows

15. February 12, 1808, Ch. Ch. MS. xlii, fol. 86; February 14, 1808, xlii, fol. 91.

16. Tuckwell, *Reminiscences of Oxford*, p. 7.

17. Robert Southey simply missed the mark when he suggested that early nineteenth-century Oxford was "a school for divinity, and for nothing else": Southey, *Letters from England*, II, 21.

very little about it."[18] Chinnery's mother had some
right to be peeved with such a tardy admission of in-
competence.

Still, apart from logic Lloyd proved to be a capable tutor. His method of obtaining the maximum
performance from his charge was a simple combina-
tion of gentle encouragement and autocratic com-
mand. First he cajoled, holding out "carrots" to en-
tice Chinnery onward. When they began the study
of advanced mathematics, he reminded Chinnery
that he himself had won a Studentship by mastering
mechanics, advanced algebra, fluxions, and three
sections of Newton all in one term. Now if Chinnery
would work equally hard, the Dean might also
honor him with a Studentship. After Chinnery failed
in his bid for a university prize on a Latin poem during his second year at Christ Church, Lloyd read the
poem and observed that it did Chinnery "very much
credit; and though you have not got the prize *this*
year, you most likely will get the next."[19] Lloyd knew
the art of gentle persuasion.

More to his nature, however, was the exertion of
blunt, authoritarian pressure. "Lloyd tells me,"
Chinnery wrote home during his last term at Oxford, "that I am vastly improved within the last
week in my quickness in calculation, which is saying
much for him: he being not naturally given to
praise: it is a principle with him that the reverse is a
better method to ensure the progress of the pupil."[20]
Lloyd's method, in short, was to demand more work

18. May 9 and May 22, 1809, Ch. Ch. MS. xlvii, fols. 117, 156-57; Oc-
    tober 25, 1809, xlviii, fol. 81.

19. November 27, 1808, Ch. Ch. MS. xlv, fol. 96; June 2, 1809, xlviii,
    fol. 6.

20. September 25, 1811, Ch.Ch. MS. liv, fol. 151.

than the pupil could do leisurely, setting the standard high in quantity as well as quality. In November, 1809, Chinnery reluctantly informed his parents that he would not have much time to write home for the remainder of the term; in fact, he had not been able to go to wine for the past three days — a sure sign of total preoccupation — because Lloyd was giving weighty assignments and making Chinnery "bear against the collar exceedingly," leaving him "really only time enough for the hours of meals and a little exercise."[21]

Such pressure made much sense to the ambitious young Chinnery, who was convinced that it was "almost impossible to insure perfection in sciences without what ... [Lloyd] calls drilling, which chiefly consists in bringing *inferences* to the mind of the student, which do not actually exist in the sciences, but of which the truth is rendered evident by theorems laid down and proved." After a few weeks of drilling, however, Chinnery began to chafe at the pressure of books to read and assignments to prepare:

> I am much inclined to think that in this learned University, we, reading men, get crammed rather than wholesomely nourished ... and I am convinced beyond a doubt that every first class man must ruminate for a whole year after he has left College — or the books which he has read will remain an undigested food upon his head.[22]

The danger of indigestion notwithstanding, Lloyd kept the pressure on.

Yet he was not the sort of tutor who stood impersonally removed from the undergraduate.

21. October 5, 1809, Ch. Ch. MS. xlviii, fol. 152.
22. December 5, 1809, Ch. Ch. MS. xlviii, fol. 166.

Despite his technique of drilling, he and Chinnery
enjoyed an informal, personal relationship in which
they conversed freely on subjects other than conic
sections. There was little of that "stiffness and
formality" which another undergraduate at Christ
Church, Charles Wordsworth, noticed between
tutors and pupils two decades later.[23] Lloyd often
appeared in his pupils' rooms unannounced,
sometimes giving assistance with a Greek verb or
mathematical problem, but more often engaging in
small talk of an inconsequential nature. A bachelor
living in close proximity to his private pupils, Lloyd
was readily available for consultation. One morning
when Chinnery ran into an impediment in the
translation of Newton from Latin to English, he "ran
to Lloyd for assistance," then returned to his rooms
to study alone for the remainder of the day.[24]

This was the world for which old Oxford men in
the late nineteenth century would pine nostalgically.
It was a time when unmarried tutors and younger
dons were not "choked with distinctions and redun-
dant with education activity" of lecturing, re-
searching, writing, and editing. It was an age when
men delighted in talking with each other: "conversation was a fine art, a claim to social distinction" as
"choice sprouts of the brain, epigram, anecdote,
metaphor" were thrown about freely. Tutor and undergraduate alike "equipped themselves at leisure
for the wit combats each late supper-party provoked."[25] With Lloyd and Chinnery, tutorials occasionally led into supper-parties. Once in May,

23. Wordsworth, *Annals of My Life*, p. 35.

24. February 28, 1808, Ch. CH. MS. xlii, fol. 156; February 7, 1810, xlix,
    fol. 25.

25. Tuckwell, *Reminiscences of Oxford*, p. 7.

1809, they planned to study mathematics for half an hour in the evening; but beginning at seven o'clock, they worked until eight, when they were interrupted by another undergraduate who came to consult Lloyd about an assignment. After the intruder departed, the tutorial proceeded for another hour, then Lloyd spontaneously had a supper brought up and invited three other undergraduates living nearby to join Chinnery and himself. Much later in the night Chinnery wrote home that the group " were merry till 11 o'clock."[26]

Tutors such as Lloyd had little difficulty finding time for frequent wine and gambling sessions, a practice which distressed the tender-minded Chinnery. Like the green freshman satirized in a popular song of the day, Chinnery had come to Oxford "a freshman so modest: The figure he cut was the oddest, all Puritan stocking and starch."[27] Once he was flattered to be invited to a dinner party thrown by a tutor, and was pleased to see Lloyd at the party. But he was shocked when whist and loo began to be played for money. He stood pathetically on the side for a while, then went to his rooms and poured out his frustrations in a letter to his "Dearest Mama": "But does it not strike you as being rather indecorous," he concluded, "that men who have taken full orders in the Church should meet in this way to play for money?"[28] Had Lloyd known of the letter, he would have been simply amused. He was scarcely sympathetic towards a puritan mentality.

While Lloyd and Chinnery continued to study and play, in 1809 Cyril Jackson, at 63 years of age, re-

26. May 31, 1809, Ch. Ch. MS. xlvii, fol. 183.

27. E.T. Cook, *The Life of John Ruskin*, 2 vols. (New York, 1911), I, 52.

28. December 6, 1808, Ch. Ch. MS. xlv, fol. 126.

tired from the Deanery and moved to Felpham on the coast of Sussex, where he lived out the remaining ten years of his life assisting and supervising his former students and friends. He was succeeded in the Deanery by Charles Henry Hall (1763-1827), predictably a Westminster School and Christ Church man, a former tutor and Censor under Jackson. Made a Canon of Christ Church in 1799, the year in which he delivered the Bampton Lectures, Hall was appointed the Regius Professor of Divinity in 1807 (a post from which he resigned when he became Dean of Christ Church). By experience he was well-qualified to take on the Deanery; but lacking Jackson's ability and energy, he was forever to remain in "the Old Dean's" shadow. Though he held the Deanery of Christ Church for fifteen years, Charles Henry Hall was not destined to be a memorable Dean.

Physically gone from the scene, Cyril Jackson remained as a presence whose high standards, Christ Church pride, and personal style were to be emulated for some time to come. Certainly Charles Lloyd was a life-long disciple. Like Jackson, Lloyd was assertive, unpredictable, buoyant. His humor was usually tinged with irony; he could be curt simply by nodding his head, and he was outspoken, often for the sheer shock effect. When Chinnery returned to Christ Church after one of his summer vacations and reported on the hefty list of books he had read during the break, Lloyd exclaimed simply "My God, you have worked."[29] Flattered, Chinnery was nevertheless rendered speechless.

Lloyd's insensitivity almost caused a complete cleavage between himself and Chinnery. A hint of

29. October 16, 1808, Ch. Ch. MS. xliv, fol. 119.

strain between pupil and tutor first appeared in a letter of October 25, 1809, when Chinnery suggested to his parents that Lloyd would probably not be his private tutor much longer: Lloyd had recently become a Master of Arts, and M.A.s were not normally allowed to conduct private tutorials. This evasion was followed by two further evasions: "I shall not regret this much I think; for I do not think that Lloyd will be of much use to me. He does not see me enough for a private tutor, and is not soundly learned in mathematics."[30] Chinnery's mother was shocked to receive the news. She had gleaned no previous hint that Lloyd's "mathematical fund" was inadequate. How could her son receive maximum benefit "from one who is *weak* in classics, and *not deep* in mathematics"? And how could Lloyd presume to take money while not giving his pupil a sufficient amount of his time? There was only one course of action logically to be taken: "Certainly it is to be hoped you may speedily get rid of him," Mrs. Chinnery wrote on October 27, 1809, "and look out for a sound mathematician."[31] Yet the matter was allowed to drag on for the remainder of the term. Upon talking with his official college tutor, Chinnery was assured that Lloyd was the best mathematics tutor in Oxford. Avoiding the issue over the Christmas holidays, Chinnery admitted to his parents that he had over-stated the inattention paid by Lloyd, and that he was actually incapable of judging his tutor's mathematical abilities. The real point of discontent remained hidden.

30. October 25, 1809, Ch. Ch. MS. xlviii, fols. 81-82.

31. Mary Chinnery to G.R. Chinnery, October 27, 1809, Ch. Ch. MS. xlviii, fol. 87.

Finally, in February, 1810, Chinnery admitted
that the essential issue was more personal than
academic. He was upset because Lloyd treated him
"like a boy, & others like men": "he calls me a boy,
and if there be a second person with me in his room
he gives up his *whole* attention to that other person."
Then came the final rationalization: "However this
does not much signify; Lloyd is not a man whom I
ever shall know in any other way but that of a
private tutor." Still, young Chinnery could not disguise his pain. Although he admitted that all his
peers at Christ Church called him "boy, or small
man, or small Chinnery," for Lloyd to address him
in that manner was something else. It was "more the
way in which he says it, if any body be present, than
the thing itself which is disagreeable."[32] Perhaps
Lloyd, himself short and overweight, was projecting
upon Chinnery some of his own feelings of physical
inadequacy.

Chinnery's mother was furious. Lloyd, she assured
her "sweetest and dearest George," must "himself be
a stupid fellow, and ill-bred, besides having very little idea of the proper mode of treating a young
man, so as to excite his energies and fire his ambition." He should henceforward be met with a
"frigidly cold but respectful" response; if he ever
again gave his attention solely to another person
while Chinnery was in the room, he should be left
with the other party and told that "as you are
engaged just now, I can just go to such a place, or

32. February 13 and February 19, 1810, Ch. Ch. MS. xlix, fols. 47, 64.
   Chinnery's size, mannerisms, and social timidity prompted his peers
   also to address him as "Miss Chinnery," or simply "Missy," and to
   tease him for his refusal to ride hacks: "his Mama sends him a hob-
   by-horse": June 4, 1808, Ch. Ch. MS. xliv, fol. 11.

do such a thing and return by the time you are at leisure."[33]

Although Chinnery never had to resort to leaving a tutorial, he took his mother's advice to heart and determined "henceforward to give up all familiarity & particular friendship with ... [Lloyd], considering him solely in the capacity of a tutor."[34] Unfortunately there is no evidence to indicate what Lloyd thought of the situation. He was probably unconscious, initially, of the uproar caused by his sardonic bantering, but surely he caught some glimmer of his pupil's hurt feelings when Chinnery refused to discuss anything beyond the academic topic for the day, made a point of dashing out as soon as the lesson was finished, and even refused an invitation to dinner. In all his letters home in the spring of 1810, Chinnery never mentioned Lloyd's calling him "boy" again. In fact, he scarcely mentioned him at all except for a petty comparison with Abraham Robertson, "a delightful beautifully slow, beautifully clear" lecturer who was, in Chinnery's estimation, "10000000000 times better than Lloyd,"[35] Throughout March and April Lloyd's name appeared in the brief daily schedule — such as "Ll. 11-12" and "with Ll. for math, 10:30" — only in the most frigid and formal terms.

Lloyd himself finally had to break the ice. In early May, shortly after Chinnery had written an English

---

33. Mary Chinnery to G.R. Chinnery, February 14, 1810, Ch. Ch. MS. xlix, fol. 52.

34. February 19, 1810, Ch. Ch. MS. xlix, fol. 64.

35. February 22, 1810, Ch. Ch. MS. xlix, fol. 69. Abraham Robertson (1751-1826), the author of the "Conic Sections" (*Sectionum Conicarum Libri VII*, 1792), was Oxford's Savilian Professor of Geometry, 1797-1810, and Astronomy, 1810-1826: XLVIII, 398.

poem in hopes of winning a University prize, Lloyd
sent him a characteristically short and blunt note:
"Dear Chinnery, come to me now and put *it* in your
pocket." Though there was no question as to what
"it" meant, Chinnery went without the poem. He
and another tutor had agreed that no one else
should see the poem before it was presented in the
University competition. Disappointed, Lloyd made
Chinnery recite the poem by heart, expressed his
delight with it, and insisted on seeing a written copy.
Chinnery, overcome with such attention, hastened to
fetch his copy. Lloyd read it several times and appeared highly impressed.[36] Henceforward the tutor
and his pupil were on the best of terms. From that
day forward there was never another squeak of complaint about Lloyd's interest or ability.

As the shadow of final examinations began to
lengthen, Chinnery increasingly relied on Lloyd's
advice. Whereas earlier he had responded unques-
tioningly to the instructions of his mother, and had
even put many of Lloyd's directives to the scrutiny
of maternal wisdom, now he came to terms with the
realities of his situation. His tutor, not his mother,
held the keys to success in the schools.

Lloyd's authoritative opinion especially came to
the fore in the autumn of 1810, when Mrs. Chinnery
began urging her son to cultivate his social rela-
tionships. Young George had studied hard during
his first two years, so why should he not now relax a
bit and form those connections which would serve
him well in later life? Somewhat naively Chinnery
asked Lloyd what he thought of the suggestion, only

36. May 10, 1810, Ch. Ch. MS. 1, fol. 2. Chinnery's poem, "The Statue of
the Dying Gladiator," won the Newdigate Prize in July, 1810:
Gentleman's Magazine, LXXX (1810), 61-62, 71.

to receive a long discourse on the ways and means of excelling in the Oxford examinations — an outright contradiction of the advice from home. "Lloyd's ideas and yours seem to be widely different on the subject of collegiate society & the cultivation of collegiate acquaintances," Chinnery wrote to his mother on October 23, 1810.

> He thinks a man should in the first part of his college career devote as much time to society as to reading; but that during the last year of his residence, he should waive all such ideas, & remain satisfied with the connections he may have formed in the first two or three years; — moreover, that it is impossible that a man should take a good degree, if he does not during that last year in a great measure exclude himself from society.[37]

For the first time, Chinnery stuck with Lloyd's advice despite his mother's wishes.

Throughout Chinnery's final year of preparation for the examinations, Lloyd served not merely as a tutor but as an indispensable ally. Chinnery stayed in college during the summer of 1811, reading Aristotle and Thucydides; in early September he became anxious for the return of friends. "Of all of them however," he wrote on September 2, "there is none whom I shall be so delighted to have by me,

37. October 23, 1810, Ch. Ch. MS. li, fol. 28.

just now, as Lloyd; for of course he will make it a point to tutorise me every day."[38] Receiving word from a friend that Lloyd would arrive on September 12, Chinnery hastened to finish his reading of Cicero and to review the *Conic Sections* before his tutor's return. But "the sooner he comes, the better," Chinnery wrote somewhat frantically to his mother. "The plot begins to thicken; every day brings me nearer to my examination, & every day adds to anxiety & hope."[39]

When Lloyd arrived at Christ Church on the evening of September 9, he went immediately to Chinnery's rooms. They chatted casually about their respective summer's activities, and early the next morning Chinnery was in Lloyd's rooms during breakfast, eager to get instructions for his mathematical studies. The grind had begun. Tutor and pupil worked together daily for at least two hours, usually more. "Lloyd is at my elbow & pressing me to fluxionise with him," Chinnery wrote home on September 15. Two days later they worked for five hours on Cicero and Thucydides. Upon learning that Chinnery was studying until well past midnight and was rising at 6 a.m. to commence again, Lloyd warned him "not to overdo the thing," offered him his horse, and insisted that he ride in the afternoons for relaxation.[40]

Lloyd's concern was not misplaced. Soon exhausted with his rigorous schedule, Chinnery began to chafe at the study of mathematics. Fluxions appeared to be an endless and tiresome "science of ap-

38. September 2, 1811, Ch. Ch. MS. liv, fol. 93.

39. September 5, 1811, Ch. Ch. MS. liv, fol. 101.

40. September 10, 12, 15, 17, 1811, Ch. Ch. MS. liv, fols. 117, 121, 127, 133.

plication which leads the mind into an endless variety of investigations," but most trying of all was "that
odious & abominably tedious book called the Conic
Sections."[41] The necessity of memorizing the hun-
dreds of mathematical demonstrations left little time
or energy for the study of ethics, logic, rhetoric, or
divinity. Why bother spending so much time on
mathematics? The practical answer was immediately
obvious: Chinnery stood a far better chance of winning a first-class distinction in mathematics than in
classics; his strength needed to be reinforced. Given
this unalterable fact, he formulated a workable
philosophy concerning the intrinsic worth of his
labors in mathematics:

> I am convinced that the Mathematics, which I am
> now reading eight or nine hours a day, have already
> strengthened my mind & though they cannot give it
> powers of *invention* they have certainly given it
> powers of tenacity. It is impossible that the mind
> should not be improved in that way if it becomes
> able, which I mean to make it, to take up well the
> *body* of Mathematics in which I shall be examined at
> the School.[42]

Though he had not the time to pursue his interests
beyond the rules and forms of mathematics, Chinnery reasoned that "on the foundation I am laying I
can hereafter raise a super-structure, & that I might

41. September 13, 1811, Ch. Ch. MS. liv, fol. 123; October 24, 1811, lv,
   fol. 53.
42. September 30, 1811, Ch. Ch. MS. liv, fol. 160. This was a common
   Oxford rationalization for laboring over material which was essentially dull. Henry Fynes Clinton, at Christ Church from 1802 to
   1805, reasoned that the value of a classical education lay in its moral
   effect — imbuing the mind with intellectual toughness — rather
   than in "the value of the knowledge required": C.J. Fynes Clinton,
   Literary Remains of Henry Fynes Clinton (1854), pp. 275-78.

not have been tempted at any future time to undergo the drudgery of learning the elements."[43] Despite the drudgery, he carried on.

Such tenacity was hardly universal at Christ Church. During the month prior to the examinations of 1811, several undergraduates dropped mathematics altogether and reconciled themselves to sitting only the classics portion of the ordeal. One of Lloyd's own pupils dropped out, informing Lloyd that he hated mathematics and was "quite disgusted with the labour of it."[44] Chinnery, on the other hand, knew himself to be on shaky ground in the classics, but was hoping for a first-class performance in mathematics — "worthy of some eminent commendation," as the statute of 1808 defined it.[45] Thus he and Lloyd worked harder as the day of reckoning approached. On the Friday before the Monday on which the examinations were to begin, they met in mid-afternoon and crammed until well past midnight.[46]

Their earnestness met with qualified success. As Chinnery had realistically expected, he got a low second class in classics — falling into the category lampooned by an Oxford wit of the day: "To call you a 'Third' would be false and absurd. But indeed I can't call you a 'Second'."[47] But he got a resounding first class in mathematics.[48] Pleased, he gave a

43. October 20, 1811, Ch. Ch. MS. liv, fol. 123.

44. October 22, 1811, Ch. Ch. MS. lv, fol. 57.

45. As one undergraduate put it, "honour and celebrity attend success in their [mathematics] pursuit": J.S. Boone, *The Oxford Spy, in Four Dialogues* (Oxford, 1819, 4th ed.), p. xxiv.

46. November 17, 1811, Ch. Ch. MS. lv, fol. 106.

47. Cox, *Recollections of Oxford*, p. 107.

48. Christ Church Collections Book, 1811, p. 449.

large dinner party for his Christ Church friends. "Lloyd too shall be among them," Chinnery wrote excitedly to his mother, "& I shall rejoice to see him partake of the festivities to the savouring of which he has so greatly contributed."[49]

Equally delighted, Mrs. Chinnery too wanted to show her appreciation to Lloyd. Now having nothing but praise for him, she suggested paying more than was customary, if it would not offend him and if the Dean of Christ Church would allow it. No doubt Lloyd could have adjusted his sense of propriety to the arrangement, but when the Dean of Christ Church declared that more money would not be in order, Chinnery decided, instead, to present Lloyd with a finely-bound book as a token of gratitude. Yet Mrs. Chinnery had the final, melodramatic word: "I quite *love* Lloyd, my dear George!" The stormy days of conflict were past; G.R. Chinnery was no longer a boy. Assisted by Lloyd, he was set on his way to a career in the Treasury.[50]

Lloyd's work with Chinnery, however, has a larger significance than the mere personal success of an undergraduate. It serves as a corrective to the impression gleaned from the activities of undergraduates such as John Jacob Buxton, who matriculated at Christ Church in 1807. Buxton's manuscript diary of 1809 portrays a pattern of University life that was a legacy from the

49. November 19, 1811, Ch. Ch. MS. lv, fol. 111.

50. Mary Chinnery to G.R. Chinnery, November 20, 21 1811, Ch. Ch. MS. lv, fols. 115, 117. Chinnery was admitted as a student to one of the Inns of Court, but never practiced. Appointed a Commissioner of Claims at Madrid, there he died unmarried in 1826: W.H. Welply, "George Chinnery, 1774-1852, with Some Account of his Family and Genealogy," *Notes and Queries* (January 29, 1927), p. 77.

eighteenth century. He rose just before noon each day, had lunch at a local hotel or inn, rode all afternoon, and spent each evening sipping wine and playing whist. No tutor intervened with onerous academic assignments. As in days of old, Oxford was simply a pleasant place to mark time before Buxton inherited his father's estate.[51]

Although such cases were still abundant in early-nineteenth century Oxford, Chinnery's type of academic earnestness was coming to be more common. One of his contemporaries at Brasenose, Henry Hart Milman, a future historian and Dean of St. Paul's, determined "to read at least a quarter of a mile every day" of his undergraduate tenure (1810-1813). Milman won the Newdigate Prize in 1812 and the Chancellor's Prize for Latin verse in 1813. He achieved first-class distinctions in classics despite the fact that all three of his Brasenose tutors proved to be incompetent: "One can lecture and never does, another cannot and always does, the third neither can nor does," Milman wrote to his parents in 1810.[52] His academic accomplishments were made in spite of, rather than because of, his tutor.

Yet the experience of three other contemporaries suggests that the work of Chinnery and Lloyd exemplified a new spirit that was entering the mainstream of Oxford life, producing a transformation of no small importance. At Corpus Christi personable, dedicated tutors, men who "excited emulation" and demanded exactness in study, assist-

---

51. Manuscript Diary of J.J. Buxton, 1809, Ch.Ch. Library MS. 466.

52. Arthur Milman, *Henry Hart Milman, D.D., Dean of St. Paul's; A Biographical Sketch* (1900), p. 22.

ed John Keble in 1806-1809, John Taylor Coleridge in 1809-1812, and Thomas Arnold in 1811-1814. Living on "the most familiar terms with each other," tutors and pupils regularly discussed modern as well as ancient literature, poetry and history, logic and philosophy, and each of the various battles against Napoleon's forces. As with Chinnery, the examinations loomed large for Keble, Coleridge, and Arnold. "We were not entirely free from the leading-strings of the school," Coleridge later noted; "accuracy was cared for; we were accustomed to *viva voce* rendering, and *viva voce* question and answer in our lecture-room, before an audience of fellow-students, whom we sufficiently respected; at the same time, the additional reading trusted to ourselves alone, prepared us for accurate study, and for our final exhibition in the schools."[53] In their willingness to give serious attention to their respective duties as student and tutor, Chinnery and Lloyd were not alone.

In the second decade of the nineteenth century Oxford graduates returning to the scene of their past pleasures were invariably impressed with the new atmosphere prevalent among tutors and undergraduates. In 1812, J.W. Ward (later the first Earl of Dudley), after ten years' absence from the University, was "quite astonished" at the change that had taken place within a single decade. Idleness was "no longer reckoned genteel"; now it was "much more *the thing* to read than to let it alone," and it was even considered "quite discreditable to be seen lounging about at those hours that ought to be given

53. Arthur Penrhyn Stanley, *The Life and Correspondence of Thomas Arnold* (1852), pp. 7-8; cf. Coleridge, *Memoir of Keble*, pp. 11-12.

to study."[54] Although the revised examinations loomed large as an institutional factor in this change, tutors such as Lloyd formed the connecting link between the institution and the undergraduate.

As he approached his thirtieth birthday in 1814, Charles Lloyd's personality and values were firmly set. He was personable, yet possessed of a tough veneer that often appeared insensitive, sometimes cruel, to a tender spirit such as Chinnery. Energetically engaged in the performance of his academic duties, he was something of a swashbuckler, enjoying a rough-and-tumble life of the mind and expecting others to do the same.

Religiously he was of the traditional, reasonable, low-keyed High Church type, a variety of churchmanship dominant in early nineteenth-century Tory Oxford which was bereft of Catholics and protestant Dissenters, suspicious of latitudinarians, and condescendingly oblivious of the Evangelicals at St. Edmund Hall. In 1808 Lloyd was ordained, as Oxford tutors had to be.[55] He regularly attended the customary college prayers, and occasionally served in Oxfordshire parishes when called upon by ill or lazy incumbents. In July, 1810,

54. S.H. Romilly (ed.), *Letters to 'Ivy' from the First Earl of Dudley* (1905), p. 182.

55. May 19, 1808, Ch. Ch. MS. xliii, fol. 154.

he accepted the curacy of Drayton, near Oxford.
But as young Chinnery discovered to his dismay,
Lloyd was in no sense other-worldly, or "holy" in his
deportment. Neither saintly nor mystical, he
harbored no inclinations toward such virtues associated with religious enthusiasts.

An anxious streak of ambition, lying just beneath
the surface of an apparently confident exterior, occasionally made itself known. In January, 1811,
Lloyd complained to Chinnery that "the distance of
his abode from the Metropolis had in a great
measure precluded him from learning" much about
politics. For the time being, he had "no friends in
power or about to come into power & therefore no
hopes to build upon them" for ecclesiastical preferment.[56] In fact, Lloyd was being unnecessarily
pessimistic. By 1811 Robert Peel was serving under
another Christ Church man, Lord Liverpool, the
Secretary of State for War and the Colonies. As
Liverpool became the Prime Minister in 1812, Peel
was well-launched on an illustrious career in which
the power of ecclesiastical as well as political
patronage would be at his fingertips. He was not the
sort of man who would forget his former college
tutor and friend. Moreover, in old Cyril Jackson,
now retired in Sussex, Lloyd had a patron of in-
estimable value.

During each summer vacation, Lloyd visited
Jackson, shared Christ Church gossip, and occasionally reflected upon his own prospects. Shortly
after one of those sessions in 1813, Jackson received
a query from the newly-nominated Bishop of London, William Howley, concerning young clerics at

56. January 21, 1811, Ch. Ch. MS. lii, fol. 5.

Christ Church whom the former Dean would recommend for a chaplaincy. Jackson's first choice was Lloyd:

> I think that Lloyd has twenty times more sound materials in him than any of those whom I left behind me at Ch. Ch. Besides his being an excellent Classical Scholar, his Mathematics have given him a hardness of head & a solidity of thinking wch. few possess. He is one of those who always know whether his opinions are well founded or not, & when he knows them to be so, nothing will ever move him from them. He is not quite so much the man of this world as I cd. wish him to be, but there is nothing in his nature to offend or distress. His heart is capable of strong & affectionate attachment, & he wd. undergo any thing for those to whom he is attached. You will understand me in one word when I tell you that he is a man whom I have long wished (& I have wished it very strongly) to consecrate to Divinity. He is just the sort of man whom we want in the present time. And I think in the last visit he paid me, in July, I carried my point — & that he left me determined to make Divinity his real object & to pursue it steadily.[57]

Cyril Jackson was as wise and generous as he was cantankerous.

---

57. Cyril Jackson to William Howley, August 13, 1813, Howley Papers, Lambeth MS. 2186, fol. 50.

III ENTERING THE PUBLIC ARENA

FROM 1813 TO 1815 LLOYD SERVED as a University examiner, at a time when it was exceedingly difficult to
muster academic enthusiasm. The prolonged conflict with France — over 20 years of war on land and
sea — was coming to an end, and English attention
was fixed on continental affairs. Oxford dons and
undergraduates, too, were distracted.

Following Napoleon's abdication in April, 1814,
Oxford was thrown into "a flutter of excitement and
preparation" for the celebration of victory.[1] On June

1. Milman, *Henry Hart Milman*, p. 29.

14 the Prince Regent accompanied the Emperor of
Austria, the King of Prussia, and several other
foreign dignitaries in a grand visitation. As the entire town was illuminated, a sumptuous banquet was
held in the Radcliffe Library. On the following day
the royal party was received in the theatre and
honorary degrees were conferred upon several of
the visitors. Latin orations were delivered; recita-
tions of English, Latin and Greek verses followed.
Enormous crowds pushed and shoved their way
down Oxford's narrow streets as dons and
dignitaries basked in the delights of the victors'
peace.[2] But the celebrations proved to be premature. In February, 1815, Napoleon escaped from
Elba, reorganized his army, and attacked the coalition in Belgium. Not until June, 1815, was the issue
decided at Waterloo.

While all of Europe celebrated, quaked, and
celebrated once again, Charles Lloyd was hit with
personal grief. On May 26, 1814, his mother died at
the age of 54, and on September 4, 1815, his father,
aged 70, died. Both were buried in the parish
church of Great Missenden.[3] Henceforth Lloyd was
the oldest surviving member of his immediate
family.

In 1817 the interests of Lloyd and Peel coalesced.
Four years earlier Lloyd had written to his former
pupil lamenting that there had been "very little intercourse" between them since Peel "first took leave

---

2. *The Annual Register*, LVI (1814), "Chronicle," pp. 47-48;
    Mallet,*History of Oxford*, III, 213.

3. George Lipscomb, *The History and Antiquities of the County of
    Buckinghamshire*, 2 vols. (1847), II, 385.

of Christ Church,"[4] but in fact their respective worlds were vastly different. Since 1812 Peel had been serving as the Chief Secretary for Ireland in Liverpool's administration. In a clash with Daniel O'Connell he received the derisory but fitting tag of "Orange Peel." Unyielding in the face of Irish agitations, in legislation as well as in public speeches Peel dealt harshly with Irish Catholic demands for political representation. Following his opposition to a Catholic Relief Bill in 1817, he was considered the parliamentary leader of the anti-Catholic forces, standing in juxtaposition to the liberal Tory, George Canning, who was also a member of Christ Church.

Both Peel and Canning coveted an Oxford parliamentary seat, a prestigious, safe seat (usually for life), with the added sentiment attached to representing one's *alma mater*. For several years it had been rumored that Charles Abbot, one of Oxford's representatives, would soon resign his seat in order to accept a peerage. Thus sides had formed at Oxford, some for Peel, others for Canning. One visitor in 1815 noted "a strong party in Christ Church" supporting Peel.[5] Lloyd himself was a minor but vocal member of that group.

The opinion of Christ Church was crucial, since historically Christ Church controlled one of the two University seats. Because of its size and prestige, it was able to exercise "a preponderating influence" in political as well as academic affairs.[6]

4. Charles Lloyd to Robert Peel, March 14, 1813, BM Add. MS. 40225, fol. 223.

5. Heber, *Life of Reginald Heber*, I, 429.

6. Thompson, *Christ Church*, p. 188.

Once the resident members of Christ Church agreed upon a candidate and gathered a few additional votes from the authorities of the other colleges, the election was a foregone conclusion.

Abbot's resignation in May, 1817, created a flurry of debate at Christ Church. The Dean, Charles Henry Hall, supported Canning.[7] But several canons opposed the Dean on the basis that Canning had shown signs of too much independence in parliamentary matters, his soft position on the Catholic question being only one example. As Lloyd later explained to Peel, they "did not believe in the sincerity, the consistency, the honesty of the man."[8] After a hectic, tiring debate that lasted the entire day and early into the evening of May 30, the Christ Church chapter agreed upon Peel and commissioned Lloyd to deliver the message to him in person.[9]

At seven o'clock the following morning, Lloyd slipped a note into the hand of a servant at Peel's residence in London:

> My Dear Sir
> Allow me to see you directly: I am come to you express.
>
> Yours,
> C Lloyd[10]

---

7. Only a fortnight before Abbot's resignation, Hall assured Canning that he, not Peel, would receive the nomination from the Chapter of Christ Church: Gash, *Mr. Secretary Peel,* p. 212.

8. Lloyd to Peel, February 18, 1825, BM Add. MS. 40342, fol. 207.

9. See Charles Lord Colchester (ed.), *The Diary and Correspondence of Charles Abbot, Lord Colchester,* 3 vols. (1861), III, 5-7.

10. BM Add. MS. 40267, fol. 225.

The good news came as a complete surprise to Peel, though on the previous day he had written to Lloyd inquiring of the vacancy and had decided to send his brother-in-law to Oxford to gather information on the subject.[11] He had no idea that Christ Church would act so quickly. Lloyd stayed for an hour as the two men discussed the rapid succession of events which led to the nomination. A plum, coveted by both, had fallen into their laps earlier than either had anticipated.[12]

Upon returning to Oxford that afternoon, Lloyd learned that the Dean and the Senior Censor, William Corne, had made the rounds of the heads of colleges in the University, and had encountered little opposition to Peel's nomination.[13] Yet at Oriel College there was, in the picturesque words of Lord Eldon's biographer, a "mortification to find the election virtually settled."[14] When Lloyd heard the rumor that the Orielites were angry, he had a ready explanation: "[Edward] Copleston and [John] Davison are themselves very warm supporters of the Catholic Claims & have uniformly opposed the University Petitions [against Catholic Emancipation]; they are also the regular opponents of every measure wch the great body of the University have

11. Gash, *Mr. Secretary Peel*, p. 212.

12. Lloyd to Peel, June 10, 1817, BM Add. MS. 40266, fol. 329.

13. Lloyd to Peel, June 1, 1817, BM Add. MS. 40266, fol. 147. "In short," John Bull (a Christ Church tutor) wrote to G.R. Dawson, Peel's brother-in-law, "none showed any disposition to oppose us — & many expressed a determination to support us": BM Add. MS. 40266, fol. 168.

14. Twiss, *Public and Private Life of Lord Chancellor Eldon*, II, 296.

considered to tend to our honour & improvement."[15]

According to Lloyd, the Catholic question was never mentioned in the deliberations at Christ Church. Yet one is hard-pressed to separate at least a tacit concern with that issue from the minds of those Christ Church men who discussed their alternatives in terms of which candidate would most "wish well to the Church & the Constitution."[16] It is probably true, as Professor Gash has suggested, that Peel won the nomination on the basis of Canning's unpopularity rather than on "his own somewhat accidental reputation as Protestant champion."[17] But Lloyd had a more positive, flowery interpretation of the event. "You are elected," he wrote to Peel, "on the score on your high & excellent public character; on account of your manliness of conduct, alike remote from intemperance & indifference; from your attachment to the Tory Principles and the true Interests of the Church of England, as they are considered and always have been by this University."[18] Unconsciously, Lloyd was indulging in a bit of redundancy: Tory principles and the true interests of the Church of England were by now, for him, synonymous.

On the matter of Oriel's opposition to Christ Church's control of the nomination, Lloyd's staunch

15.   Lloyd to Peel, June 1, 1817, BM Add. MS. 40266, fol. 149.
16.   *Ibid.*, fols. 149-50. Years later Lloyd was still insisting that the Catholic question had nothing to do with Canning's rejection: Lloyd to Peel, February 18, 1825, BM Add. MS. 40342, fols. 207-8; and Lloyd to Peel, April 22, 1827, BM Add. MS. 40343, fol. 59.
17.   Gash, *Mr. Secretary Peel*, p. 216; cf. Colchester, *Diary and Correspondence*, III, 7.
18.   Lloyd to Peel, June 1, 1817, BM Add. MS. 40266, fol. 145.

Christ Church pride emerged. Confident that Peel would contribute to the University's "honour and improvement," Lloyd was most of all pleased that the nomination had "done more for the honor of Christ Church than has been done in some years. It is merely by constantly determining not to propose any one to the University who is not in all respects unobjectionable, that Ch Church will always be allowed to have one of the Members out of her own body."[19] The reference to his old college prompted Peel to respond in an intensely personal, reminiscent vein:

> I treat you as I should my father or my brother, [and] consider all your zeal and all the warmth of your attachment, so natural — so like what I experienced some nine or ten years since, when I was aspiring to a distinction in the University, which I coveted then almost as eagerly as I have since coveted another and a higher distinction — that I forget to thank you, or at least feel assured that you are as sensible of my gratitude as I am of your kindness.[20]

Such candid sentiment, though infrequent in the voluminous correspondence between Peel and Lloyd, was certainly not out of character in their relationship. Earlier Lloyd had noted that the nomination meant for Peel "the high object of a noble & honourable ambition," while to Lloyd himself it was "the object of my dearest wishes & most anxious hope."[21] Characteristically, the idea of ambition was couched in terms of nobility and honor; and in the

19. Lloyd to Peel, June 5, 1817, BM Add. MS. 40266, fol. 207.
20. Peel to Lloyd, June 9, 1817, BM Add. MS. 40266, fol. 279-80.
21. Lloyd to Peel, June 5, 1817, BM Add. MS. 40266, fol. 149.

larger significance of Lloyd's "most anxious hope,"
one is reminded that the ambition was not confined
to Peel.

Following Peel's nomination, Lloyd became his ad-
visor and confidant in all matters pertaining to the
University. On June 1, 1817 (the day after his return
to Oxford), he wrote no fewer than three letters to
Peel, and he averaged a letter a day for the next
week, fastidiously serving as a barometer of opinion
at Oxford.

Unfortunately Lloyd was susceptible to unnecessary alarmism, as was evident in his insistence
that an official contradiction should be given to *The
Morning Chronicle*'s suggestion that Peel's candidacy
was an anti-Catholic measure concocted by the
Liverpool cabinet. Suspecting that the rumor
originated among the Canningites at Oxford, Lloyd
viewed the report as "a very insidious one; there is a
mixture of truth & falsehood in it, which might do
mischief (in my opinion & it is only my own opinion
that I send you) unless it be explicitly contradict-
ed."[22] Peel wisely decided to dismiss the advice. Five
years in Ireland had hardened him against
journalistic abuse, and he and Canning simply had a
good laugh over the article.[23] The falsehood so

22. Lloyd to Peel, June 1, 1817, BM Add. MS. 40266, fol. 149.
23. Parker, *Peel*, I, 252.

much outweighed the truth, he explained to Lloyd, that any sensible person could tell the difference.[24]

Lloyd was most helpful in advising Peel on the traditional, unwritten details to which a candidate for Oxford had to attend. He suggested that Peel should resign his present seat on the day before the announcement of the Oxford election and as Dean Hall wanted Peel to make the rounds of the colleges on the eve of the election, Peel should write to Cyril Jackson in order to find out what one was expected to do and say on such a trek.[25] After the election a University official would relay the news to London and should be paid the customary fee of ten guineas. There would be no other immediate costs for the taking of the seat, except fees for the bell-ringers.[26] Soon, however, Peel would need to give fifty guineas to the Radcliffe Infirmary, making him a governor — traditional for a representative of the University. For the formal note of acceptance following the election, Lloyd again had advice: "it ought to be *short, respectful* & *thankful* and altogether good. Do not let the beginning of it be formal. I am not sure that it will be seen in Convocation; indeed I imagine not; but it will certainly be seen by many persons."[27] As one obeying his father or older brother, Peel followed Lloyd's instructions to the letter.

Traditionally a candidate did not show his face at Oxford on the day of the election. But Peel, wanting to see friends, inquired of Lloyd if it would be "perfectly proper & respectful" to arrive on the day

24. Peel to Lloyd, June 2, 1817, BM Add. MS. 40266, fol. 151.
25. Lloyd to Peel, June 5, 1817, BM Add. MS. 40266, fol. 206.
26. Lloyd to Peel, June 1, 1817, BM Add. MS. 40266, fol. 147.
27. Lloyd to Peel, June 8, 1817, BM Add. MS. 40266, fol. 275.

of the election rather than on the following weekend, as his duties in Ireland might require a hasty departure.[28] Lloyd's reply was immediate and definite: "It might look a little like unnecessary display" for Peel to appear before the weekend. "I hope," Lloyd added, "you will not be obliged to go over to Ireland; what good can you do unless you take a fleet laden with corn over with you? If however there be disturbances, I suppose you will be wanted to quell them. But don't fight O'Connell ... "[29] In sharp contrast to Lloyd's instinctive grasp of the details of Oxford formalities was a total lack of comprehension of the Irish situation. On the question of avoiding a fight with O'Connell, Peel replied simply that "it would be a much more difficult matter to have that satisfaction than you are probably aware of."[30]

Taking Lloyd's advice, Peel did not appear in Oxford until the weekend after the election. On Saturday morning, June 14, the two men had breakfast together in Lloyd's rooms at Christ Church. Primarily they discussed their mutual responsibilities, Lloyd pledging himself as a channel of information on any University matter that would be of importance to Peel, and urging his former pupil to send the Dean of Christ Church copies of all the official correspondence sent from Peel to the Vice-Chancellor of the University.[31] The interests of Christ Church had to be guarded carefully, particularly since Oriel's recent challenge. Apparently the two men talked of the future, for Lloyd gave an uncannily prophetic

28. Peel to Lloyd, June 9, 1817, BM Add. MS. 40266, fol. 278.
29. Lloyd to Peel, June 10, 1817, BM Add. MS. 40266, fol. 329.
30. Parker, *Peel*, I, 253.
31. Lloyd to Peel, June 12, 1817, BM Add. MS. 40267, fol. 11.

assessment of Peel's prospects as a representative of
the University:

> You are elected by the University younger than has
> ever before fallen to the lot of anyone; and as
> hitherto has been the uniform conduct of the
> Univy., elected for life. Something very strong, at
> least, must occur before this ancient precedent will
> be broken through. But you are also almost the only
> man who has had at the time of his election a strong
> hand on Politics. It depends therefore I think entire-
> ly on yourself whether there shall ever be any in-
> disposition in the Univy. to break thro' this prece-
> dent...
> Now Oxford, it may without argument be as-
> sumed, will never vary from the principles of Mr.
> Pitt; the attachment to them seems to be at this place
> to increase with time. So far then I think certain any
> person who is a strenuous defender of these prin-
> ciples will hold this seat for ever. Now I would simp-
> ly ask, whether any man of 29 years old can say
> positively that if he is left entirely to his own single
> opinion, this never can happen during the space of
> 40 years, which is (you see) the time I allow you to
> sit as our Representative. But if you are a member of
> the Administration founded entirely on these prin-
> ciples, your own prejudices will coincide with all
> your best principles & your conduct never can
> change.[32]

Here is an example of what Cyril Jackson meant
earlier when he noted that Lloyd was "not quite so
much the man of the world" as he could wish him to
be. Although one's principles might remain un-
altered, one's conduct would certainly need to be adjusted to fit the changing times. Little did Lloyd
foresee that whereas Peel's Pittite principles — an in-

32. Lloyd to Peel, n.d. (June, 1817), BM Add. MS. 40267, fol. 227.

stinctive emphasis on tradition, order, and authority
which allowed for moderate but not radical reform
— would remain the same, the implementation of
those ideals would change. Nor would Lloyd himself
be so stolidly fixed "for ever" in his own brand of
Oxford Toryism.

For the time being, however, Lloyd acted in good
Tory fashion in attempting to protect Oxford
University from the changes envisaged by liberal reformers. The University, like the aristocracy and the
Church on which its position was established, was
under fire in the years following the Napoleonic
Wars. Oxford was seeing, as Professor Ward suggests, "the perils as well as the advantages of
adherence to the establishment" and was itself fully
exposed "to the dangers which threatened all
privileged corporations in an age of criticism and reform."[33] In 1817 publishers were agitating against
the copyright law which required them to send a
free copy of every new book to eleven libraries, including the Bodleian. The long-established privilege
of Oxford and Cambridge stood in need of defense.
Various compromises were proposed by members of
each university. Despairing over the prospects of being able to retain the Bodleian's privilege, Frodsham
Hodson, Principal of Brasenose, suggested that
Parliament should grant Oxford and Cambridge
£500 *per annum* for the maintenance of their
libraries. Lloyd was horrified with the implications of
Hodson's proposal:

> I individually think that it is always better not to ac-
> cept anything of this kind from Parliament. The
> Bodleian hitherto has been founded & repaired & re-

33. Ward, *Victorian Oxford*, p. 40.

newed continually by private Benefactions & the annual contributions of the members of the University. If Parliament shall give us £500 pr. Ann. how long will it be think you before some worthy Mr. Bennet will use this grant as an argument for the interference of the Commons in the management of the Library? how long will it be before they send us an order to open our Library on such days & at such hours as shall suit their high & mighty pleasure? The argument has already been made use of against the Church, for which nothing worse ever was done than the annual grant of £100,000.[34]

Rather than simply offering his opinion on the issue, Lloyd collected historical information and logical arguments to put at Peel's disposal,[35] and he suggested influential witnesses from Oxford to appear before a Commons committee in the Spring of 1818.[36] The Commons committee reported, however, that only the British Museum should retain copyright privileges and that the other libraries, including the Bodleian, should be granted a fixed sum for the purchase of books. Fortunately for the University, the report was released too late in the session to be embodied in legislation, and the whole copyright issue was lost in the social and political crises of 1819 and 1820. Ironically, radical agitations served to protect the interests of Tory Oxford.

Yet Oxford was by no means out of trouble. At the same time that the copyright question was being aired in 1818, Henry Brougham, the liberal Whig, was insisting that the endowments of the Oxford colleges should be investigated by a parliamentary com-

34. Lloyd to Peel, December 24, 1817, BM. Add. MS. 40272, fol. 240.

35. Lloyd to Peel, February 8, 1818, BM Add. MS. 40273, fol. 296.

36. Lloyd to Peel, May 3, 1818, BM Add. MS. 40276, fol 283.

mittee.[37] In February, 1818, Peel asked Lloyd for
some references to the beneficial effects of university
education.[38] Lloyd not only sent a list of books, but
also outlined some ideas on the subject. "Pray don't
let Brougham's Education Bill pass the Lords," he
wrote to Peel in May. "Everybody is frightened at
these predatory commissioners."[39] In the end, the
Tory government blocked Brougham's inclusion of
the universities in his investigation, but Peel suffered
one of his few humiliations in the parliamentary debate with Brougham in 1819.[40] Whatever information Lloyd had sent him on the subject apparently
did not help.

While concerning himself with the questions of endowments and copyrights, Lloyd continued to
enlarge his place of importance at Christ Church.
On May 12, 1818, he was made Librarian of the college, and on the same day was appointed Junior
Censor, replacing Edmund Goodenough, his former
tutor who was appointed Senior Censor in place of
William Corne (who had died eight days earlier).[41]

37. See *Hansard,* XXXVIII (1818), 605-6.
38. Peel to Lloyd, February 25, 1818, BM Add. MS. 40342, fol. 18.
39. Lloyd to Peel, May 17, 1818, BM Add. MS. 40277, fol. 88.
40. See Ward, *Victorian Oxford,* pp. 46-47; and Gash, *Mr. Secretary Peel,* p. 246.
41. Christ Church Chapter Minute Book, 1802-21, pp. 229, 240.

The appointment to Junior Censor was especially satisfying to Lloyd, as the Censors were usually selected from the ranks of Westminster, not Eton, men. More importantly, in the normal course of events Lloyd would become Senior Censor, an office which promised further preferment in the Church. Yet Lloyd was not one to bide his time in the queue of ecclesiastical preferment. In May, 1818 he became Curate of Binsey, just west of Oxford. Within a week of his new appointments at Christ Church, he heard the rumor that William Van Mildert was resigning his preachership at Lincoln's Inn. As Regius Professor of Divinity at Oxford and Canon of Christ Church since 1813, Van Mildert needed to devote more time to his academic responsibilities, and he might even be in line for a bishopric. Upon hearing of the potential vacancy, Lloyd set his sights on Lincoln's Inn. Had he not been Oxford's Select Preacher in 1816? And had he not preached often and well at St. Mary's, gaining "a great degree of estimation" as a preacher? He contacted Cyril Jackson on the subject and received a three-page reply of encouragement. Jackson informed him, however, that such an appointment was no simple matter. The Benchers of Lincoln's Inn would have to be canvassed by influential friends, privately and immediately.[42]

Peel, of course, was the first friend to be contacted. The preachership of Lincoln's Inn was "the greatest testimony that can be given to the character & ability of a clergyman," Lloyd wrote on May 18, "& has always been an object very much sought after." Would Peel render his assistance? In a long

---

42. Lloyd to Peel, May 18, 1818, BM Add. MS. 40277, fols. 93-94.

letter Lloyd defended himself against the charge of
raw ambition: "I assure you very honestly that shd. I
be a candidate it will not be from my own estimate of
my powers, but in obedience to the opinions of those
to whom I have a right to bow." If Peel were of the
same opinion, his patronage would be invaluable:

> I am presenting myself for an office for which those
> to whom not only myself but the whole University
> here are wont to pay the greatest deference, esteem
> me qualified; and upon these qualifications, or
> rather upon these opinions the propriety of your ex-
> ertions must depend. But upon your applications
> and those of my other friends my chance of success
> entirely rests.

Enclosing a list of Benchers, Lloyd even noted the
three or four rival claimants to the preachership.
John Davison of Oriel College was probably the most
serious opponent. "But as the Benchers want some
one not only to preach to them, but to live with
them & be pleasant with them, Davison is not in
these latter points, at all, the person to suit them."[43]
In all modesty, Lloyd considered himself the perfect
man for the task.

　　Equally enthusiastic, Peel replied that he would
stop at nothing within his power "to promote the object" that Lloyd had in mind. "If I tell you how sincerely I wish you success," he continued, "and how
earnestly I will cooperate with you to promote it, I
shall offend that honorable and manly pride,
superbiam quaesitam meritis which would I know com-
pel you to reject every effort of private friendship
that was not equally stimulated by a conviction of

43. *Ibid.*, fols. 93-96.

your qualifications for any appointment for which you may be a candidate."[44] By now Cyril Jackson had written to Peel, recommending Lloyd. It appeared as if this network of friends was about to help obtain a most desirable post.

Yet Lloyd, characteristically nervous, was considering all the problems as well as the prospects. He had second thoughts about leaving Oxford, particularly since he had just been made a Censor at Christ Church. If there were the "slightest chance of any bustle," he would not abandon Christ Church just now. Nor did he want to put himself forward for Lincoln's Inn without "a strong chance of success."[45] On May 24 he went to London and talked personally with Peel, then traveled on to Felpham, Sussex, to consult with Cyril Jackson. Lately it had appeared to Lloyd that Jackson was being "very mysterious" on the subject of Lincoln's Inn.[46] In fact, Jackson probably had inside information that Van Mildert would not, after all, resign his preachership. Despite all the rumors, Van Mildert continued to wear the two hats of Regius Professor of Divinity at Oxford and Preacher of Lincoln's Inn. Apparently Lloyd's efforts had come to naught.

In the following year (1819), however, Van Mildert was made the Bishop of Llandaff. When he resigned his preachership, the machinery for Lloyd's success was ready to be set into motion. The one likely rival, Reginald Heber, did not stand a chance, despite his having several influential friends in Lon-

44. Peel to Lloyd, May 19, 1818, BM Add. MS. 40265, fols. 219-20.
45. Lloyd to Peel, May 19, 1818, BM Add. MS. 40277, fol. 112.
46. Lloyd to Peel, May 24, 1818, BM Add. MS. 40277, fol. 200.

don.[47] The news of Lloyd's appointment almost preceded the public announcement of Van Mildert's resignation, causing rumors to fly thick and fast. Heber's supporters, suspecting political chicanery, pointed out Peel's personal interest in the career of his old tutor. Yet when Van Mildert heard the gossipy accusations, he was amazed that anyone should question the fact of political influence; most ecclesiastical and political appointments came in that manner, even his own.

Having known Lloyd personally at Christ Church since 1813, Van Mildert was pleased with the appointment. He considered it a "point of delicacy" not to interfere with the selection of his successor. "But I have no hesitation in telling you confidentially," he wrote to H.H. Norris on March 29, 1819, "that I consider Lloyd as the man most preeminently qualified for the situation. His principles are excellent, his judgment sound, his taste correct, his learning various and extensive, his manners engaging."[48] Reginald Heber, after all, was an Evangelical, a position which evoked suspicion if not open hostility within High Church circles.[49] Whereas Lloyd often said of Van Mildert that orthodoxy oozed so freely from his pores that he probably recited in detail the doctrines of the Church of England in his dreams,[50] Lloyd's own orthodoxy — although not so

47. Thomas Taylor, *Memoirs of the Life and Writings of the Right Reverend Reginald Heber, D.D. Late Bishop of Calcutta*, 2 vols. (1836, 3rd ed.), I, 90.

48. Edward Churton, *Memoir of Joshua Watson*, 2 vols. (1861), I, 273.

49. See W.J. Baker, "Henry Ryder of Gloucester, 1815-1824: England's First Evangelical Bishop," *Transactions of the Bristol and Gloucestershire Archaeological Society*, LXXXIX (1970), 134-35.

50. Churton, *Memoir of Joshua Watson*, I, 282.

provocative of imaginative description — was unquestioned.

The period of Lloyd's preachership at Lincoln's Inn, 1819-1822, was such an uneasy time in the social history of the English people that the challenge of the Evangelicals appeared inconsequential compared to the radical threats facing the established order. Orthodox churchmanship and the English aristocracy stood side by side, both under duress. Since the war, trade had declined; wages had fallen, factories were closed, and unemployment was alarmingly high. Not without cause was the country "in bad humour," as J.W. Ward suggested.[51] Throughout the kingdom restless, angry mobs were rioting, raiding shops, breaking machines,and railing against established authority. Even Peel, who was not one to be unduly alarmed, confided to Lloyd that he feared "a revolution at no great distance — not a bloody one & perhaps not one leading to a republic, but one utterly subversive of the aristocracy and of the present system of carrying on the Government."[52]

Shortly after Lloyd took up his new post at Lincoln's Inn, the infamous "Peterloo Massacre" occurred near Manchester. But radicalism was not confined to the midlands. In 1820 two events in London were doubtless too close for Lloyd's comfort. One was the bizarre Cato Street Conspiracy, in which several radicals plotted the assassination of the entire Liverpool Cabinet, only to have their conspiracy betrayed by a government informer. The

51. Ward, *Letters of Dudley to Llandaff* p. 158.
52. Aspinall, *Three Diaries*, p. 118.

executioner's platform had hardly been dismantled before the fiasco of George IV's divorce proceedings against Queen Caroline provided another occasion for massive mob gatherings and hooliganism. Unfortunately we have no record of Lloyd's reflections on these matters, nor do we have the texts of any of his sermons preached at Lincoln's Inn during this chaotic period. One can be sure that he had no sympathy for the radicals. Newman later said more than met the eye when he recalled that Lloyd considered himself "the official expounder of the Christian Religion and the Protestant faith" to those lawyers who laid down "peremptorily the law of the land" through the courts.[53] The "multitude," Lloyd later noted, was "so rude and so little spiritual" that they could not grasp the nuances of the Christian religion.[54]

While at Lincoln's Inn, he came into contact with the London ecclesiastical scene. The Bishop of London was William Howley, the future Archbishop of Canterbury whom Lloyd had come to know at Christ Church when Howley was Regius Professor of Divinity there from 1809 to 1813. Also in London was the promising young Charles James Blomfield (a future Bishop of London), vicar of St. Botolph, Bishopsgate. With Blomfield's reasonable, orthodox churchmanship outweighing his Cambridge background in Lloyd's estimation, the two men became close friends shortly after Lloyd arrived in London.[55]

53. J.H. Newman, *Autobiographical Writings,* ed. and introd. by Father Frank Tristram (New York, 1957), p. 70.

54. *The British Critic,* 3rd ser., I (1825), 104.

55. Lloyd to Peel, January 17, 1827, BM Add, MS. 40343, fol. 4.

More importantly, as far as Lloyd's expanding circle of friends was concerned, Van Mildert introduced him to Joshua Watson, a prosperous wine merchant retired at Clapton, known for his charitable deeds and outspoken commitment to the old High Church party; and to Henry Handley Norris, the incumbent at Hackney who supported most of the High Church societies, contributed money and manuscripts to *The British Critic* (the leading High Church organ of the day), and dispensed a large portion of his private fortune on ecclesiastical projects. Norris and Watson formed the core of a group of orthodox Anglicans who were nicknamed the "Hackney Phalanx" or the "Clapton Sect" (an allusion to the rival Evangelical group, the "Clapham Sect"). In unison these men held to the authority of the creeds and liturgies as defined in the ancient church, were opposed to the individualism and emotional outbursts associated with Evangelicalism, and emphasized the sacraments rather then preaching.[56] Lloyd felt at home in their midst.

On February 21, 1820, he was elected to the membership of a men's dining club in London, the "Nobody's Club" (later the "Nobody's Friends Club"). Founded in 1800 by William Stevens, the club was an eccentric gathering of lawyers, ecclesiastics, writers and academics. According to the by-laws, the composition of the membership was one-half clergy and one-half laity. Watson, Norris, and Van Mildert were members, as was Francis Randolph, a Cambridge theologian.[57] The group dined together regularly, engaged in intellectual repartee,

56. See Francis Warre-Cornish, *The English Church in the Nineteenth Century*, 2 vols. (1910), II, 70-73.

57. J.A. Park, *Memoirs of the Late William Stevens* (1859), p. 126.

and shared each other's concerns. Here was a common-room atmosphere transplanted from the cloisters of Oxford and Cambridge. Van Mildert was a member, as his biographer cogently put it, "to his no small mental gratification, not to say his future advantage in life."[58] And so was Lloyd.

Yet Lloyd was by no means severed from his former friends and concerns. Despite his living most of three years in London, his connections with Christ Church remained intact. He necessarily resigned the Censorship (on September 17, 1819),[59] but as he had neither married nor obtained a cure of souls, he was entitled to keep his Studentship. Moreover, he was allowed to retain the office of Librarian of Christ Church. With a Sub-Librarian performing most of the ordinary duties in his absence, Lloyd occasionally returned from London to Christ Church in order to attend meetings and to keep abreast of the workings of the Library. No doubt he availed himself of the opportunity to keep his Oxford friendships and reputation in repair.

In London he continued to serve as Peel's sounding-board and informal tutor. Early in 1819 Peel wrote to him inquiring of "the best specimen, not exactly of reasoning, but of that part of reasoning which is occupied in confutation of your adversary's arguments." Wanting to form "some general principle of arguing and reply," Peel found Locke too brief and Chillingworth too ponderous. He suspected that the best reasoning could be found in theological writers, and wished to know if Lloyd would guide his investigation. "I do not want to read

58. William Van Mildert, *Sermons on Various Occasions, and Charges* (Oxford, 1838), "Memoir of the Author," by Cornelius Ives, p. 20.

59. Christ Church Chapter Minute Book, 1802-21, p.249.

for information on the subject; at least that is not my chief object. What I want is subtle reasoning in reply. I care not if the book is on alchemy."[60] Surely Lloyd had something better than alchemy to offer.

He also had advice, as well as a ready ear, for Peel on the question of English currency. Early in 1819 Peel was nominated chairman of the parliamentary committee whose function was to inquire into the complex problem of cash payment of wartime debts and the efficacy of paper currency. With little experience in financial affairs, he consulted Lloyd — determined to deal with the issue, as he put it to Lloyd, "with the same attention with which I would read the proof of a proposition in mathematics."[61] Partly due to their collaboration, a parliamentary bill ("Peel's Act" of 1819) set into motion the gradual return to the gold standard. Although there is no need to over-state Lloyd's importance in this matter, his influence was certainly present throughout. Not only did his mathematical tutelage stand Peel in good stead, but he also served as a constant reference point, ready to hear, criticize, and advise.

While consulting with Peel and enlarging his own social group within the ecclesiastical sphere, Lloyd apparently did a creditable job as Preacher at Lincoln's Inn. The Archbishop of Canterbury, Charles Manners-Sutton, was sufficiently impressed to recruit him as his Domestic Chaplain. Rarity of rarities in this appointment: Lloyd was chosen for

---

60. Parker, *Peel*, I, 289.

61. Parker, *Peel*, I, 291-3. For the details of this intricate currency problem, see Élie Halévy, *The Liberal Awakening 1815-1830*, trans. E.I. Watkin (New York, 1961), pp. 49-52; cf. Gash, *Mr. Secretary Peel*, pp. 239-45.

the post without any solicitation by himself or his
friends.[62]

In 1819 Lloyd first tried his hand at publication,
when he reviewed Charles James Blomfield's
*Dissertation upon the Traditional Knowledge of a
Promised Redeemer* for *The British Critic*.[63] As a friend
and fellow High Churchman, he extravagantly
praised Blomfield's "amazing fund of erudition, the
profound scholarship, and the acuteness of practised
criticism"; he predictably hailed the appearance of
Blomfield as a theological writer "not only on account of the excellence of his work, but because his
appearance here is itself a thing *optimi exempli.*"[64]

Amidst the generalities and Latin phrases in
Lloyd's first published essay, three themes stand out
as indicative of his orientation. The first, characteristic of his High Church heritage, had to do with
the importance of the testimony of the ancient
church. Lloyd credulously agreed with Blomfield
that the angel which appeared to Moses was the
second person of the Trinity, simply because "this
was the unanimous opinion of antiquity, and we see
no reason to depart from it." A second theme was a
pedagogical, donnish concern for material which
would be useful to students of divinity. Lloyd was
pleased with Blomfield's citations because they could
be "of the greatest service to the theological students." And finally, he revealed his interest in
foreign — especially German — theology: Blom-

62. Peel to Lord Liverpool, January 18, 1827, BM Add. MS. 38195, fol.
    193.

63. The article was unsigned, but Lloyd's authorship was revealed in a
    letter from W.R. Lyall to Edward Burton, January 4, 1830,
    Shrewsbury School MS., II, fol. 1.

64. *British Critic* XII (1819), 653.

field's notes at the end of the treatise, Lloyd suggested, would be "useful not only for the purpose of elucidating the several arguments on which they bear, but for referring the reader to many celebrated works of foreign Divines, from which they may derive information on some of the most important topics of Divinity."[65]

There was no novelty in the emphasis on antiquity. Most Oxford clerics, other than the few beleaguered Evangelicals at St. Edmund Hall, would have instinctively made a similar point. Nor is one surprised to find Lloyd seizing upon the educational value in Blomfield's treatise. Having spent his entire life in the presence of schoolmasters and dons, it is remarkable that he saw much else. But the line concerning the "works of foreign Divines" is noteworthy, given the pronounced insularity of Oxford theologians in the early years of the nineteenth century. Only a few years earlier Edward Tatham, Rector of Lincoln College, had preached a two-and-a-half-hour sermon quaintly consigning all the "Jarman" Biblical critics to the bottom of the "Jarman Ocean."[66] Oxford men who were not hostile to German theology were largely unaware that it existed. Lloyd's note in *The British Critic* was a portent of his own role in bringing some awareness of those "foreign Divines" to England.

In 1821 another of Lloyd's reviews was published in *The British Critic,* and again Blomfield was involved. Blomfield's censure of a thesaurus translated by E.H. Barker and A.J. Valpy had provoked

---

65. *Ibid.,* pp. 657, 660.
66. Cox, *Recollections of Oxford,* p. 220. n. 1.

Barker to reply in *Aristarchus Anti-Blomfieldianus*,[67] the book reviewed by Lloyd. The entire issue was so recondite that the editor of *The British Critic* totally misquoted Barker's title when he later identified Lloyd as the author of the review.[68] Yet the essay once again revealed something of Lloyd's perspective. Fittingly, he was impressed with Blomfield's criticism of Barker because it was so logical and mathematical:

> The censure was indeed of that kind which compels assent: it was not derived from the principles of probability or taste, but deduced by a regular train of reasoning, and proved by the strictest rules of logical and arithmetical calculation. The mind was not at liberty, in reading it, to say "this is true" " that is not true": the most anxious friend of Mr. Valpy and Mr. Barker must have been compelled to admit the truth of Dr. Blomfield's strictures, unless they were prepared at the same time, as is possible, to deny the truth of any proposition in the mathematics.[69]

Standing cold in the face of "principles of probability or taste," Lloyd never felt the need to disguise the fact that he was a child of Newtonian mathematics rather than Wordsworthian sensibility. Certainly on the conscious level the romantic movement missed him altogether.

The quantity of Lloyd's output was as unimpressive as its quality. He wrote only one other article (in *The British Critic*, 1825), edited some sixteenth-century formularies (1825), produced a

67. See *The Quarterly Review*, XXII (1820), 302-48.

68. Lyall referred to Barker's book as "Aristophanes contra Blomfieldicum": Lyall to Burton, January 4, 1830, Shrewsbury School MS. II, fol. 1.

69. *British Critic*, XV (1821), 192-93.

Greek New Testament for his students (1827) and a Book of Common Prayer with red-letter rubrics (the first in England) published posthumously in 1829.[70] This rather meagre record, by a man deemed to be one of Oxford's leading scholars in the twenties, was characteristic of the age. In the thirties and forties a publication-mania swept over Oxford (largely from polemical motives), as exemplified in the work of Newman, Keble, Pusey, and their kind. But during the first three decades of the century the University was certainly no hive of scholarly activity.

This lack of literary zeal can be explained, in part, by the size and character of the University in the early nineteenth century. The circle of scholars was so small and homogeneous that men knew what others were doing and thinking. In the words of R. W. Church, "Oxford was a place where every one knew his neighbour, and measured him, and was more or less friendly or repellent; where the customs of life brought men together every day and all day, in converse or discussion; and where every fresh statement or every new step taken furnished endless material for speculation or debate, in common rooms or in the afternoon walk."[71] With Oxford as insular as it was informal, the arduous task of publication was deemed unnecessary for the dissemination of ideas or the demonstration of one's abilities.

Yet other factors were at work. Most tutors were very young, and professors (usually without college

70. Anonymously Lloyd also wrote *A Dialogue between Parson Ives and his Man David* (1822), a S.P.C.K. tract "For the counteraction of infidel and blasphemous publications." I am grateful to Mrs. Deborah Thomas for this information.

71. Quoted in B.A. Smith, *Dean Church: The Anglican Response to Newman* (1958), p. 23.

connections) were few in early nineteenth century Oxford. A tutor's normal ambition was to marry and obtain a college living on which to support a growing family, a scheme for which the writing of learned reviews, articles and books was not particularly advantageous. One's interests were far better served by attending to the teaching and administrative demands of one's college, or by forming beneficial connections with some other patron and waiting patiently for a living to become vacant.

Professor and tutors alike saw themselves too consumed with college and university chores to bend their minds to scholarly penmanship. Even the Regius Professor of Divinity, William Van Mildert, took this line of reasoning. Asked in 1818 to recommend some Oxford friends who might contribute to a new journal, *The Christian Remembrancer,* Van Mildert replied to the editor that most of the men whose services might be of use to the journal were "too deeply engaged in the business of tuition, or in official concerns of the University." The problem, according to Van Mildert, was one of priorities. "When we recollect," he added with a hint of self-congratulation, "the prodigious number of those who go forth from these sequestered abodes of learning, to contribute their share to the welfare and preservation of the community, perhaps [the dons] are doing as much substantial good as if they were to abate some of their attention to their pupils for the purpose of joining in literary warfare."[72]

Van Mildert's explanation would be plausible were it not for the fact that subsequent generations of Oxford and Cambridge academics have found the time

72. Churton, *Memoir of Joshua Watson,* I, 278.

and summoned the energy to write as well as teach and serve on college and university committees. In truth the level of scholarly expectation was low in the early nineteenth century. Gentlemen scholars were gentlemen first, and often not scholars at all. Afternoon strolls or rides, heavy high tables, much port and common-room banter left little place for scholarly pursuits, even if the interest in writing had been present.

Lloyd himself had other interests. He instinctively knew that his ecclesiastical prospects would be enhanced by keeping up his political connections rather than by turning out literary treatises. Hence the nibs of his pen were worn not with the writing of scholarly essays, but with his correspondence with Peel. Over-nervous, he was often in a fretful or manipulative mood, hardly a creative state of mind. Yet one thing is certain: Lloyd's problem was certainly not the one which was attributed to Cyril Jackson. According to a Christ Church graduate, Jackson refused to commit his thoughts to the printed page because he was so filled with "literary vanity" that he shrank "with timidity from the eye of criticism."[73] Charles Lloyd was not one who hid his talents under a bushel.

73. Beste, *Personal and Literary Memorials*, pp. 215-16.

IV THEOLOGY IN A NEW KEY

WHILE SERVING AS PREACHER at Lincoln's Inn, Lloyd maintained his connection with Christ Church not only by retaining his Studentship and Librarianship, but also by exchanging the latter office in the spring of 1820 for the more important Wake Librarianship.[1] Momentarily absent, he was not forgotten. When the Regius Professorship of Divinity became vacant in the summer of 1820, the entire Chapter of Christ Church recommended Lloyd for the nomination. Wanting one of their own members

1. Christ Church Chapter Minute Book, 1802-21, p. 256.

in the canonry attached to the chair, they were openly displeased when the Liverpool administration appointed Frodsham Hodson, the Principal of Brasenose. Himself disappointed, Lloyd remained hopeful for future consideration when he was informed by Robert Peel that he too had unreservedly supported his candidacy.[2]

On January 18, 1822, Hodson, only 51 years of age, died suddenly after a short illness. Three days later the Dean and Chapter of Christ Church met to consider a request submitted earlier by Lloyd. Having been granted the living of Bersted, in Sussex, a "peculiar" of the Archbishop of Canterbury (no small favor by a Primate who was a Cambridge man), Lloyd had applied for special permission to retain his Wake Librarianship while holding the incumbency. As they granted the request, surely the Dean and Chapter suspected that the recent death of Hodson made their decision an empty formality.[3] In all probability, Lloyd was soon to return to Oxford as the occupant of one of the most coveted chairs in the kingdom.

Unforgetful of the ill-will caused by the appointment of Hodson two years earlier, Lord Liverpool (himself a Christ Church man) was eager to assuage the feelings of the largest college at Oxford. After making the perfunctory "necessary enquiries respecting the persons best qualified to hold the situation," he reported to King George IV that John Davison of Oriel and Lloyd of Christ Church were the two most likely candidates. Both men seemed "thoroughly qualified for the situation from their

2. Peel to Lloyd, August 4, [1820], BM Add. MS. 40269, fol. 36.

3. Christ Church Chapter Minute Book, 1822-35, p. 5.

abilities, character, and learning in Divinity in all its
branches." But Liverpool inclined towards recommending Lloyd, whose appointment would "give
most satisfaction to the University at large, and
particularly to Christ Church, of which the Divinity
Professor is a cannon [sic]."[4]

In early February, 1822, Lloyd's appointment was
announced publicly.[5] Shortly thereafter he resigned
as Wake Librarian, and was installed as Canon of
Christ Church; his Studentship was naturally
voided.[6] When he resigned his preachership at Lincoln's Inn, however, the Benchers circulated a petition requesting him to remain as their chaplain
while performing his duties as Regius Professor at
Oxford. Van Mildert, they insisted, had held both
offices before he took the episcopal see of Llandaff
in 1819, and Lloyd had an assistant who could handle most of the duties at Lincoln's Inn. Following the
failure of the first petition, the Benchers submitted
another, but to no avail.[7] Lloyd stood firm in his decision to resign, a stance which struck Reginald
Heber (himself pleased that he might now obtain the
post which eluded him in 1819) as being "extremely
incredulous."[8]

Certainly no motives of ecclesiastical reform
prompted Lloyd to refuse to play the pluralist game.
He simply did not want to divide his attention
between Oxford and London. Happy to return to

4. Arthur Aspinall (ed.), *The Letters of King George IV, 1812-1830,* 3 vols.
   (Cambridge, 1938), II, 499.

5. *Jackson's Oxford Journal,* February 2, 1822.

6. Christ Church Chapter Minute Book, 1822-35, p. 6.

7. Peel to Lord Liverpool, January 18, 1827, BM Add. MS. 38195, fol.
   193.

8. Heber, *Life of Reginald Heber,* II, 54.

the University under such prestigious conditions, he felt the need to give himself completely to theological studies, without diversions. He intended to make a name for himself, to revive theological studies at Oxford, and possibly even to found a new school of theology.[9] Moreover, he was now facing the necessity of settling down. He was engaged to be married.

Apparently it was in London that Lloyd met Miss Mary Harriet Stapleton, the second daughter of Colonel John Stapleton of Thorpe Lee, Surrey, but no evidence is available on the precise time and circumstance of their initial acquaintance. On August 15, 1822, they were married in Thorpe Lee parish church.[10] Deciding that the canonical house provided at Christ Church was unsatisfacory, they moved into the rectory of Ewelme, a parish several miles from Oxford attached to the Regius chair of Divinity. From Ewelme Lloyd commuted by horse and carriage to his duties at the University.

Within ten months of the wedding, a son was born and was baptized at Ewelme by Lloyd himself on August 14, 1823. Annually for the next three years a child was born.[11] Well could Lloyd congratulate a friend, J.W. Whittaker, on his marriage in June, 1825, and hope that the Whittakers' union would be "as full of happiness and comfort as my own — and that Whittakerians [?] may appear as fast as the little Lloydicles have done."[12]

9. Lloyd to Peel, February 28, 1826, BM Add. MS. 40342, fol. 329.

10. *Jackson's Oxford Journal,* August 24, 1822.

11. Bodl. MS. ODP d. 283: Parish Register Transcripts, Ewelme 1813-1900.

12. Lloyd to J.W. Whittaker, June 24, 1825, Bodl. MS. Top. Oxon. d. 314, fol. 71.

The professorial stipend which fed and clothed
this expanding circle of little Lloydicles came from a
variety of quarters. The financial structure of the
eighteenth-century establishment — in this case the
collegiate clergy — had hardly altered by 1822. Still
the revenue came largely from land, more or less
directly; the amount varied annually, usually for the
better if the land was "improvable." The entire
system was, in Professor Best's words, "ex-
traordinarily complicated and haphazard."[13] Lloyd's
stipend was drawn from a general Fund for Christ
Church canons, derived from siga (small rents from
estates in Oxfordshire, Cheshire, and
Worcestershire), rent of some rooms in Christ
Church, tithes from livings near Oxford attached to
Christ Church, various fines (money paid by tenants
for leases), labor at annual audits, rents from Christ
Church meadow, profits from timber sold off land
owned by the college, and coal royalties.[14] In 1824
the total was roughly £1500 per year.[15]

Lloyd's expenses were similarly varied. In 1822 he
paid £27.7 window tax, spent £10.6 on wines, and
gave small amounts to various needy groups such as
the poor in Bridewell, the prisoners in the Castle,
and the poor in St. Bartholomew's Hospital. Frequent subscriptions were raised at Oxford for the
hungry and unemployed in times of bad crops,[16]

13. G.F.A. Best, *Temporal Pillars: Queen Anne's Bounty, the Ecclesiastical
    Commissioners, and the Church of England* (Cambridge, 1964), pp.
    62-63.

14. Ch. Ch. MS. xxxvii. b. 54: Dr. Lloyd's private accounts, 1822-1829.

15. Lloyd to Peel, December 10, 1824, BM Add. MS. 40342, fol. 173.

16. Cox, *Recollections of Oxford*, pp. 92, 110-11.

and Lloyd usually gave something each time. In his position he could hardly avoid solicitations. He was even approached by Bishop Hobart of New York who was traveling in England in 1824 soliciting funds for the new General Theological Seminary in New York City. Lloyd contributed £2, as he noted in his personal account book, "for the purpose of the general Theological Seminary instituted for the education of the Ministry in the American Episcopal Church."[17]

All the while he had his own family expenses. As H.H. Norris was preparing to pay the Lloyds a visit in 1826, he received a letter from Lloyd requesting that a cook be brought from London. "Pay twenty or twenty-five guineas; the first would be as suitable as the second; but, as they say, we will not quarrel about the difference. Kitchen maid? Yes. Quiet family. Madame scolds? Not much. Must be able to dress a good dinner. Academics like to feed well."[18] Evidently academics also liked to drink well: in 1825 Lloyd spent £82.10 on port and sherry.

Of greater importance than his personal affairs, however, was his public labor as the Regius Professor of Divinity at Oxford. Within seven years, from 1822 to 1829, he transformed the teaching of theology and impressed himself — in his techniques of instruction as well as the content of his theological

17. Ch. Ch. MS., Lloyd's private accounts; cf. G.F.A. Best, "Church Parties and Charities: The Experience of Three American Visitors to England 1823-1824," *English Historical Review*, LXXVIII (1963), 243-62.

18. Churton, *Memoir of Joshua Watson*, I, 286-87.

perspective — upon the memory of an entire generation of Oxford ecclesiastics.

Entailing few specific duties, a professorship at Oxford around the turn of the nineteenth century amounted to a type of sinecure. Examples are as numerous as they are notorious. In the 1790's the Lady Margaret Professor of Divinity lectured but once a term, and the Savilian Professor of Geometry was forever non-resident, sending a deputy. In 1809 *The Edinburgh Annual Register* reported that only nine of twenty-three professors in the University offered any courses of lectures, and not all of them were able to attract a hearing of undergraduates.[19] Charles Dyson, Rawlinsonian Professor of Anglo-Saxon from 1812 to 1816, lectured only once during his five-year stint — "one admirable lecture, and one only, he delivered."[20] Thomas Gaisford, Regius Professor of Greek from 1811 to 1831, never delivered even one.[21]

The Regius Professors of Divinity were somewhat more diligent. Though their lectures were uninspired and abysmally boring, they were at least given with some regularity. According to a University Statute, divinity lectures were to be delivered at 9 a.m. each Monday and Friday on some part of the

19. Ward, *Victorian Oxford,* pp. 8, 16.
20. Coleridge, *Memoir of John Keble,* p. 37.
21. Cox, *Recollections of Oxford,* p. 167, n. 1.

Scriptures; the Professor himself was to give a series of lectures at least one term each year. All candidates for the M.A., unless they were students of law or medicine, were required to attend; a candidate for the B.D. degree had to attend the lectures of the Regius Professor for seven years, and a candidate for the D.D. was required not only to attend, but also himself to lecture in Latin and on the Scriptures.[22] The practice, however, was not in keeping with the rules. Most divinity lectures at Oxford, in fact, were attended only by young men who were preparing for holy orders,[23] as before ordination most bishops merely required a certificate from the Regius Professor indicating that the candidate had attended the lectures satisfactorily.[24]

The quality of divinity lectures left much to be desired. John Randolph, the Regius Professor of Divinity from 1783 to 1807, is invariably cited in the memoirs of Oxford men as a typical example of the low state of affairs in the early nineteenth century. Ignoring the statute governing the day and hour of lectures, Randolph delivered his gems of wisdom by candlelight at seven o'clock each Sunday evening during Lent Term. The class, having had dinner at 3 p.m., desserts at 4, surplice-prayers at 5, and tea at 6, were inevitably in a drowsy state. The darkened room allowed sleep to go undetected, and Randolph's lectures seldom served as an interruption. Years later one of his listeners could recall "only the monotonous drawl and air of *procuranteism* and indifference" with which the lectures were delivered. Oc-

22. William Ince, *The Past History and Present Duties of the Faculty of Theology in Oxford* (Oxford, 1878), pp. 38-39.

23. Coleridge, *Memoir of John Keble*, p. 401.

24. Beste, *Personal and Literary Memorials*, p. 221.

casionally there was a bit of drama injected when Randolph stopped in the middle of a sentence and glared intently at a late-comer who had to enter the door directly behind the Professor's desk. Then Randolph returned to his notes and droned on until he posed the stock philosophical question, "Why does God not prevent the existence of evil?" Even his handling of this issue reminded one listener of a master mason in Lincolnshire who, peeved with a mistake made in the construction of a wall, said to his journeyman: "There you stand, as *unconsarned* as if you had nought to do wi' it." The man of the cloth, Randolph, like the man of the trowel, was "engaged in handling subjects familiar and habitual."[25]

The effect on students was predictable. Attendance was irregular at best. Boredom reigned, as no questions or examinations accompanied the lectures. No special classes were held, nor was there ever any comment on that "sleep-compelling ceremony." "In short," Cox noted, "the only things really carried away by the majority of the class, were the Syllabus given to each one at the commencement of the course and a formidable printed list of authors recommended for future reading, presented at the close of the lectures."[26] There is little wonder that the High Church mainstream of the Anglican clergy were so ill-prepared, theologically, to cope with either the Evangelical or the Tractarian challenges.

Yet John Randolph, bad as he was, at least made

25. *Ibid.,* pp. 221-22. Randolph (1749-1813) was also Regius Professor of Greek, 1782-83, and Professor of Moral Philosophy, 1782-86; in 1799 he was consecrated as Bishop of Oxford, translated to Bangor in 1807 and to London in 1809.

26. Cox, *Recollections of Oxford,* p. 131.

an impression which rendered him memorable. One
is hard-pressed to find any contemporary references
to the activity of his successors, Charles Henry Hall
(1807-9) and William Howley (1809-13), though admittedly their tenures were brief. Apparently Van
Mildert (1813-20) was more diligent. In a letter to
Henry Hobart in 1820, H.H. Norris noted some recent improvements in English society and a renewal
of religious interest within the Universities: "Our
universities, Oxford especially, have been repairing
the decays of discipline and of the requisite
knowledge for their degrees; and competent
knowledge of the evidences and principles of Christianity is made indispensable to every one."[27] Quietly
Van Mildert had been doing a commendable job.

But it is to Lloyd that the historian of Oxford's
theological faculty looks as the key person who "gave
fresh life and vigour to the Public Lectures, which
had fallen into comparative disregard."[28] As Canon
Liddon put it, Lloyd "soon made his Chair more of a
power in Oxford than it had been under any of his
predecessors, not excepting Van Mildert."[29] This he
did by lecturing regularly, energetically, and im-
aginatively.

Commencing in the spring of 1823, Lloyd explained that his purpose was to "begin at once to
furnish the student with rules [i.e. principles] for
conducting his theological enquiries."[30] He distribut-

27. John McVicar, The Early Life and Professional Years of Bishop Hobart,
    (Oxford, 1838), p. 492.

28. Ince, History of Theology in Oxford, p. 25.

29. H.P. Liddon, Life of Edward Bouverie Pusey, 4 vols. (1893-97), I, 62.

30. E.S. Ffoukes, A History of the Church of S. Mary the Virgin, Oxford, the
    University Church, from Domesday to the Installation of the late Duke of
    Wellington, Chancellor of the University (1892), p. 400.

ed the customary reading list, then plunged into a lecture on the Old Testament. Subsequent lectures were on the New Testament, early ecclesiastical history, atheism, deism, natural and philosophical "evidences of Christian religion," and "controversial divinity" (Arianism, Socinianism, and Unitarianism). The term was ended with two sessions devoted to the Protestant Reformation.[31] Each year the lectures were revised; new topics were added as some were deleted, and the sequence was shuffled. Occasionally an entire term was given to a single Biblical or historical topic.

Biblical studies, largely ignored in an Oxford that knew more about Homer than St. Paul, were given a boost by Lloyd. According to E.B. Pusey, who took copious notes on the public lectures, Lloyd early began introducing some objections to the Mosaic authorship of the Pentateuch. But for Pusey a series of lectures on the Epistle to the Romans was the best instruction on "not so much the full meaning of the Holy Scripture, as how to study it." Lloyd's method was to deal with only three or four verses each hour, examining each word, both in its own meaning and with reference to the context. Then he traced the various interpretations of the text in the history of Christian theology, emphasizing the controversies it had aroused and concluding with an assessment of its present position within the Church's teachings. This thorough treatment of the Scriptures made a lasting impression on the stolid mind of Pusey. Almost fifty years later he remarked that he and his generation gleaned from Lloyd's lectures on the Epistle to the Romans "a very different idea of read-

31. See *Ibid.*, pp. 401-4, for the lecture topics.

ing the New Testament from any that we had had before."[32]

Lloyd's suggestions on the use of an interleaved Bible also appealed to young Pusey. In response to a friend's query on the pursuit of theological studies, Pusey cited his mentor's proposals in detail:

> The use of the interleaved Bible accg to Dr. L. is that when you meet with an occasional explanation of a passage, in an authour [sic] who is not a professed commentator, you may be able to set it down against the passage; & so recur to it at any time. Whereas otherwise the chances are, that you mt. never meet with it again, or not at the time you wanted it. It is not his wish that we shd. always set about filling the book at any given time, but that we shd. always have it by us to deposit in it what we may happen to fall in with.[33]

There is no doubt that Pusey, if not his friend, followed Lloyd's advice to the letter. A large floppy interleaved Bible was Pusey's trademark to the end of his days.[34]

In his reflections on the theological struggles of the Reformation era, Lloyd made a notable impression on his students. Particularly concerned with the conflict of doctrines in the sixteenth century, he insisted that the Roman view of justification depended on "the quantum of righteousness in a man," while justification in the Protestant sense meant the acknowledgment of sin and trust in Christ "for acquittal." The Reformers, according to Lloyd,

32. Liddon, *Pusey*, I, 62-63; cf. Thomas Mozley, *Reminiscences chiefly of Oriel College and the Oxford Movement*, 2 vols. (1882), I, 177-78.

33. E.B. Pusey to Richard Salwey, August 18, 1824, Pusey MS. Chest A, Drawer 7.

34. See Liddon, *Pusey*, I, 64.

defined the term "sacrament" and used the term
"*paenitentia*" equivocally, at times meaning repentance while at other times having the sacrament of
penance in mind. The Roman Catholics, on the
other hand, tended to oppose *opus operatum* to *solam
fidem,* but "never allowed that this excluded the need
of a right disposition of mind."[35]

Lloyd himself was equivocal in his assessment of
Roman Catholic theology. Generally positive in his
attitude, he was still staunchly Protestant in the old
High Church sense. Whereas he was sure that "no
great mischief was done" by Rome's insistence that
the Vulgate was authentic — "they meant only that it
might be trusted for all main points, not that it was
to be set up against the original" — he nevertheless
taught that the greatest error of the Council of
Trent lay in their putting the Apocrypha on the
same level with canonical Scripture.[36] In a preface to
some formularies which he published in 1825, Lloyd
went even further in refusing to give much credence
to anything before the Reformation of Edward VI
when "the errors of Popery were formally re-
nounced, and the pure doctrines of Protestantism
authoritatively established in this kingdom." Under
the tutelage of Cranmer, the Anglican formularies
represented "the first dawnings of a brighter day"
following that "darkness, which had so long obscured the genuine form of Christianity."[37] Here
Lloyd was showing his true Protestant colors — an
un-reconstructed bias. Taken out of context, his line
on the "darkness" of the Middle Ages sounds re-

35. Churton, *Memoir of Joshua Watson,* I, 274-76.

36. *Ibid.,* p. 275.

37. Charles Lloyd (ed.), *Formularies of Faith put forth by Authority during the
   Reign of Henry VIII* (Oxford, 1825), "Preface," pp. iv-v.

markably similar to the perspective of Joseph
Milner, the popular Evangelical historian.
In his lectures on the relation of Biblical and
natural theology, Lloyd suggested that "the different
systems of evidence" were independent of each
other and therefore cumulative in their effect.[38] Yet
he gave little attention to modern ecclesiastical history, as Pusey explained to Richard Salwey, because
he held that "ignorance on those points, (so that we
do not presume to dogmatize upon them) can hardly ever be so painful & is not so much a duty, as the
knowledge of the evidences of the fundamental doctrines of Christianity."[39] Concerned as he was to present a well-rounded theological orientation to his
students, Lloyd emphasized Biblical studies, the ancient church, and the Reformation. Medieval patterns of thought were noticeably absent, and treat-
ments of rationalist theology were skimpy indeed.
   Lloyd's students certainly did not detect any skim-
piness in the reading list they were given. His
syllabus, [40] largely of books now forgotten, staggered
many a young divinity student in the 1820's. A long
list of books from the hands of a professor was common at Oxford, but for Lloyd to demand that the
books be read was another matter altogether. In
1823 John Henry Newman found himself "too much
engaged" preparing for Lloyd's class to do much of
anything else.[41] Pusey saw the syllabus as "a track,
not a groove,"[42] but when he sent the list to a friend
who was away from Oxford studying theology in-

38. Liddon, *Pusey*, I, 64.

39. Pusey to Salwey, n.d. (1824?), Pusey MS., Chest A, Drawer 7.

40. See Ffoukes, *History of S. Mary the Virgin*, pp. 401-4.

41. Newman, *Autobiographical Writings*, p. 195.

42. Pusey to Salwey, August 18, 1824, Pusey MS., Chest A, Drawer 7.

dependently, he carefully marked the items which
were most important in order to prevent the
theological novice from despairing at the bulk.[43]
Hurrell Froude, attending the public lectures in
1826, admitted simply that Lloyd's "immense
catalogue of books" frightened him "beyond
measure."[44] Froude wrote to his father on 9
February 1826:

> Loyd's [sic] lectures will last 3 weeks longer than I
> supposed; they seem the production of a very
> superior person, & their drift is not [to] unfold a
> system of Divinity but to direct our theological
> studies; but he has so overwhelmed me with the im-
> mense mass of knowledge wh he seems to require, &
> the enormous quantity of books wh he considers
> necy, that I have [given] up any hope of putting his
> advice into effect though I shd live till there were 4
> figures in the number of my years.[45]

Still, Lloyd's public lectures were better only in
degree, not in kind, from those of his predecessors.
He would have hardly made much of an impact had
he not come up with some innovative method of re-

43. Pusey to Salwey, n.d. (1824?), Pusey MS., Chest A, Drawer 7.

44. [R.H. Froude]. *Remains of the Late Reverend Richard Hurrell Froude*,
    [eds. John Keble and J.H. Newman], 2 parts, 2 vols. in each part
    (1838-39), pt. 1, vol. i, 195. Henceforward reference will be made to
    vols. I-IV.

45. R.H. Froude to Robert Froude, February 9, 1826, Oratory MS.

viving theological studies at Oxford. Within a year after he came to the Regius chair, he began meeting with small, informal classes of select students. "I am beginning," young Newman wrote to his mother in November, 1823, "to attend some *private* lectures in divinity by the Regius Professor, Dr. Charles Lloyd, which he has been kind enough to volunteer to about eight of us."[46] To private sessions in his rooms at Christ Church, Lloyd invited the most promising young men of that generation — Newman, Pusey, Froude, Robert Wilberforce, R.W. Jelf, W.R. Churton, Edward Churton, Frederick Oakeley, Edward Denison, Thomas Mozley, F.E. Paget, and George Moberly, to name a few. Attendance was strictly by invitation, and "to gain admission," Froude reported to his father, "great interest is made."[47]

In those private classes the full force of Lloyd's eccentricity exerted itself. He was forever "walking up and down, as he lectured conversationally to his pupils, like the great Stagyrite, so that no pupil was out of earshot of his master."[48] It was a rough and

---

46. Anne Mozley (ed.), *Letters and Correspondence of John Henry Newman during his Life in the English Church*, 2 vols. (1891), I, 82. The italics are mine. College "lectures" similar to tutorials were already common in subjects other than divinity. In 1803 Thomas De Quincey (failing to distinguish between University and college lectures) noted that an Oxford "lecture" was no "solemn dissertation" as in German universities, but was rather "a real drill, under the excitement, perhaps, of personal competition, and under the review of a superior scholar": Thomas De Quincey, *Memorials and Other Papers*, 2 vols. (Boston, 1856), I, 164. A recent scholar has noted that by the 1830's it was difficult "to draw the line between a lecture for a few college men and what we should call a tutorial": W.A. Pantin, *Oxford Life in Oxford Archives* (1972), p. 42.

47. R.H. Froude to Robert Froude, February 2, 1826, Oratory MS.

48. Ffoukes, *History of S. Mary the Virgin*, p. 404.

tumble scene, where minds clashed and presupposi-
tions were challenged, "where the lecturer rather
converses than dogmatises, and the pupils feel
themselves at liberty to propose to him as many difficulties as he is benevolent enough to receive."[49]
Decked out in a long, loose-fitting coat resembling a
dressing gown, Lloyd carried a colorful pocket-
handkerchief and constantly indulged in his snuff-
taking as he sat down, bounced up, and roamed
about the room without ever losing the thread of
conversation. Such a spectacle could scarcely fail to
impress young parsons-to-be. Years later Frederick
Oakeley remembered Lloyd "making the circuit of
his large class once and again, and accosting its
several members, or those at least whom he might
choose to select, with a question which in its turn
formed the handle of a reply of its own, full of information conveyed in a most attractive form."[50]
During one of those sessions Hurrell Froude, sitting
slightly hidden behind one of his comrades, scribbled his impressions in a note to his father:[51]

> I am in one of Lloyd's divinity lectures wh he makes
> amusing by his good natured way of keeping fellows
> up to their work. We, about 20 fellows, sit all about
> in his library, wh is a very large room, & he walks up
> and down in the middle; sometimes taking his sta-
> tion before one fellow & sometimes before another
> asking them questions quite abruptly to catch them
> being inattentive, & amusing himself with kicking
> their shins. When any fellow happens to make a silly
> remark he laughs at him without the least scruple &

49. L.M. Quiller-Couch (ed.), *Reminiscences of Oxford by Oxford Men,
   1559-1850* (Oxford, 1892), p. 325.

50. *Ibid.,* p. 328; cf. Churton, *Memoir of Joshua Watson,* I, 274.

51. R.H. Froude to Robert Froude, April 18, 1826, Oratory MS.

exposes him in the most ludicrous way, but so very
good naturedly that it is impossible to be the least of-
fended. Sometimes he pulls the ears of the men he is
very intimate with. Most of the class are firsts and
double firsts. The greater part of them are masters
of arts, & a proproctor contributes his dignity to the
honours of the august assembly.

The personal touch, rough-hewn as it was, was
seldom lacking in Lloyd's relation to his pupils:

> The first communication I had with him [Froude
> continued], took place as follows. He stopped short
> in one of his walks just where I was sitting, & said
> "Well sir what am I to call you, Froude or Frowde,"
> & when I told him he said, "Then I find I used to be
> mistaken in what I used to call the Archdeacon.[52] I
> used to say Archdeacon Frowde; well then Froude
> will you please go on."

Nor could Lloyd's tendency to engage in sarcastic
banter ignore an opportunity to poke fun at Oriel
College:

> Old Wilberforce has been late two or three times, &
> [during] the last lecture old Loyd [sic] did not ob-
> serve him come in, but observing him soon after he
> called out "Well Mr. Wilberforce & when did you
> come; last again I suppose, yes I thought so keeping
> up the Oriel charter."

Little wonder that Lloyd had a reputation of being
a bully.[53] Often when he received a bright or well-
documented answer to one of his questions, he
asked sardonically if the student had received a letter on the subject.[54] Such bullying occasionally won

52. Robert Hurrell Froude (1770-1859), Archdeacon of Totnes, Devon.

53. R.H. Froude to Robert Froude, April 18, 1826, Oratory MS.

54. Quiller-Couch, *Reminiscences of Oxford Men,* p. 328.

premature converts to his way of thinking: Hurrell
Froude once noted in his diary that he had come
under Lloyd's domineering personality to such a
degree that he had "assented fully to Lloyd" on a
point on which he had actually not made up his
mind.[55] Newman, also bullied by Lloyd, later saw
method in that murderous technique: "Lloyd bullied
me as being an Evangelical," Newman reminisced to
Canon Liddon half a century afterwards, "as in truth
(Newman laughed) I then was."[56] From his
Evangelical heritage Newman brought to Oxford the
conviction that the Pope was the Antichrist, the Man
of Sin predicted by Daniel, St. Paul, and St. John.[57]
There is little doubt that he, like Frederick Oakeley
and a Mr. Woods, was called to attention by Lloyd's
hammering style. "D'ye see?" Lloyd expostulated as
he gave one of his swift kicks on the shins, "I suppose, Mr. Woods, you have been taught from your
cradle upwards that it is the special duty of a Christian to abuse the Roman Catholics;" then with
another dramatic kick, "That, d'ye see? I hold to be
a mistake."[58]

Despite the gruff exterior, Lloyd's students quickly
discovered that just beneath the surface was a sense
of good will and personal affection. Newman knew
that as Lloyd assaulted his Evangelical views, he was
at the same time taking a personal interest in his development, lavishing attention "expressive of vexation and impatience on the one hand and of a liking

55. Froude, *Remains*, I, 48.

56. H.P. Liddon's manuscript record of a conversation with Cardinal
    J.H. Newman, June 5, 1883: Pusey House, Oxford.

57. J.H. Newman, *Apologia Pro Vita Sua: being a History of his Religious
    Opinions* (1883), p. 7.

58. Quiller-Couch, *Reminiscences of Oxford Men*, pp. 328-29.

for him (Newman) personally and a good opinion of his abilities on the other." In his private journal he noted that he felt "very conceited" that Lloyd had "kindly taken notice" of him, though those probing questions undermined any sense of intellectual superiority.[59] Froude, on the other hand, was peeved that Lloyd did not pay him more attention.[60] The more the apparent abuse, it seems, the more did Lloyd's students read it as a sure sign of favor.

The sensitive, ever-critical Froude, in fact, was the pupil who recorded the most ambivalent response to Lloyd's tutelage. The lectures, though "clever and learned," did not seem to Froude "to get at anything."[61] While one of the lectures had "the beneficial effect of making things attended to wh wd otherwise be passed over without notice," to Froude's mind it came "to nothing satisfactory."[62] Lloyd impressed him as "a very clever man," but his expositions were delivered too elegantly at one point, too antithetical at another — "a style wh diverts my attention from the matter to the talent of the man."[63]

This last accusation demands further considera- tion. Did Lloyd's flamboyant style merely draw at- tention to himself, away from the subject-matter? There is no question that the style as well as the theological content of the private lectures fills the anecdotal memoirs of the former members of the class. But in fact the lectures and the lecturer were

59. Newman, *Autobiographical Writings,* pp. 71, 196.

60. Froude, *Remains,* I, 30, 33.

61. R.H. Froude to Robert Froude, October 30, 1826, Oratory MS.

62. R.H. Froude to Robert Froude, October 5, 1826, Oratory MS.

63. R.H. Froude to Robert Froude, February 2, 1826, Oratory MS.

seen to be inseparable; the method and the message
were fully integrated. Upon sending Richard Salwey
a summary of the lectures, Pusey noted his doubt
that it would be "of much use to any who have not
attended the lectures themselves."[64] In dialectical
fashion, Lloyd drew out the implications of matter-
of-fact dogma and ecclesiastical history. The snuff-
taking, shin-kicking, and ear-pulling tactics were
stage-props, dramatic techniques employed to bring
ancient theology to life. They revealed Lloyd to be
very much "consarned."

The subject-matter itself was certainly not inconsequential. It was in these private classes that Lloyd
turned the attention of fledgling Anglican
clergymen to the historical development of the
liturgy. In his own Prayer Book he had made
copious marginal notes,[65] and he in turn had several
imitators as a result of the private lectures. Combin-
ing a word study with historical analysis, he traced
the English liturgies right back through the Roman
missals and Breviary to their original sources.[66]
Whereas in the public lectures he largely ignored
the Middle Ages, in these private sessions he gave
full attention to the medieval liturgy. Of all his work
at Oxford, this was perhaps the most important in its
bearing on the future character of Anglican
churchmanship.[67]

"I am working as hard as possible in my professorship," Lloyd wrote to Peel in February, 1824,

64. Pusey to Salwey, n.d. (1824?), Pusey MS., Chest A, Drawer 7.

65. W.J. Copeland's manuscript "History of the Oxford Movement"
    (1881): Copeland Papers, Pusey House, Oxford: Vol. II, fols. 73-74.

66. Froude, *Remains,* I, 221; Quiller-Couch, *Reminiscences of Oxford Men,*
    pp. 177-78.

67. See the third section of Chapter VIII: "Lloyd's Legacy."

"&, I hope, doing some good."[68] Peel too had reason to hope that Lloyd was doing some good, for in the same year an anonymous tract was addressed publicly to Peel, inquiring about the theology being taught and the discipline being inculcated at Oxford and Cambridge. Lamenting that the present system did not adequately prepare a young man for a parish, the writer insisted that the clergy should be "a distinct and sacred class" unspotted by the vice and frivolities of the secular world. The greatest need was for specialized training, something beyond Aristotle, Locke, and Newton. Whereas a young barrister-to-be went to the Inns of Court and medical students trained in hospitals, there was no provision for divinity students to study theological, liturgical and pastoral matters in any "strictly professional and technical" way. Seeing General Theological Seminary in New York City as "a suitable and encouraging model," the anonymous author proposed the creation of theological colleges at Oxford and Cambridge; if such colleges did not do an effective job of training the English clergy, a third, ecclesiastical, university should be founded.[69]

With historical hindsight one can see that these anonymous proposals were not so far-fetched. Durham University was founded in 1832 largely for the purpose of training Anglican clergymen, and in the second half of the nineteenth century several colleges more inclined to theological studies were founded at Oxford and Cambridge. In the 1820's,

68. Lloyd to Peel, February 23, 1824, BM Add. MS. 40342, fol. 153.

69. *An Enquiry into the Studies and Disciplines, adopted in the two English Universities, as preparatory to Holy Orders in the Established Church: in a Letter Respectfully Addressed to the Right Hon. Robert Peel* (1824), pp. 21, 28-31.

however, Lloyd was working within a system which
he had inherited. Given the obvious limitations of
that system, his efforts were notable indeed. Even a
writer for the whiggish *Edinburgh Review* in 1826
mentioned "with sincere pleasure" those "zealous
and able exertions of the individual who now fills the
divinity chair at Oxford." Particularly impressed
with the innovative private lectures, the reviewer was
struck with the melancholy fact that Lloyd's work
"only benefits the few."[70]

Lloyd himself was aware of this limitation. Thus
he collected, prefaced, and published his *Formularies
of Faith* in 1825 with the express purpose of "putting
into the hands of the clergy treatises valuable for
their reading matter, and of such rare occurrence as
to be found only in public libraries, or in the private
collections of the curious." As he explained the
original reason for those formularies being
published by authority during the reign of Henry
VIII, Lloyd obviously had one eye glued to the present scene: the formularies were designed not simply
as a rejection of Papal authority, but also "to quiet
and assuage" the "variety of opinions, which, if un-
checked, might degenerate into licentiousness."[71]

Lloyd's correspondence in the mid-twenties re-
veals him to be alternately striking the pose of the
priest who dispenses encouragement and the pro-
phet who presents himself as the oracle of truth. In
1825 he sent Peel one of his sermons, inviting comment.[72] Peel, clever as he was, had not revamped the
Evangelical assumptions on which he had been

70. *Edinburgh Review*, LXXXVIII (1826), 509.
71. Lloyd, *Formularies of Faith*, "Preface," p. iii.
72. Lloyd to Peel, December 8, 1825, BM Add. MS. 40342, fol. 291.

reared. Thus he noted that "sincere repentance" was necessary for God's forgiveness if one was to avoid "inevitable and severe Punishment," and added that he certainly did not believe that all priests had the power of absolving sin.[73] Lloyd replied immediately and gratefully to the comments, but added: "I must needs tell you that in regard to the great Doctrine of Xnty you are little better than a heretic."[74]

In 1825 Lloyd also counselled H.H. Norris on the latter's place within the Church of England. He affectionately addressed Norris as "My dear Patriarch," insisting that his care for the Church was more than an archbishop's. Norris denied the title, lamenting that he was a mere watch-dog of orthodoxy, and that his role was neither sufficiently challenging nor worthy of praise. "A fig for your disinterestedness!" Lloyd replied. How could a patriarchate be a place without profit? Did not the glory of the Patriarch once eclipse the greatness of the Roman Pontiff himself? "And suppose a patriarch was only a great watch-dog! Is a dog only to bark? This, doubtless, is a great quality, and useful withal: but is he not to fight upon occasion? And has not your Holiness fought? A fig for your modesty!"[75] As usual, Lloyd's blunt manner and sharp tongue were put to good effect.

For Norris he had more than bantering encouragement. Recently Norris and Joshua Watson had assumed joint editorship of *The British Critic*, and now Lloyd — upon request — poured out ad-

---

73. Peel to Lloyd, n.d. (December, 1825), BM Add. MS. 40342, fols. 293-94.

74. Lloyd to Peel, December 23, 1825, BM Add. MS. 40342, fol. 295.

75. Churton, *Memoir of Joshua Watson*, I, 279, 282.

vice for the running of the journal. He suggested
popular articles on divinity for the country
clergymen, heavier theological and historical
treatises "for the learned, and for the character of
the Review," general material ("learning in the pro-
fane line") for the amateur scholar, accounts of
voyages and Foreign travels, a few articles on
English literature, and occasional pieces on
metaphysics, political economy, and chemistry. On
the question of contributors, Lloyd suggested that
Norris should seek out "leading men" in each
speciality, and "not give scholarship to be reviewed
by a mere theologian, or theology to a mere
scholar." Specifically he recommended Van Mildert,
Blomfield, James Henry Monk (Regius Professor of
Greek at Cambridge), W.H. Coleridge, and Edward
Burton as men whom the editors would do well to
solicit for manuscripts.[76]

Lloyd himself contributed an article, "Views of the
Roman Catholic Doctrines," which was published in
The British Critic in October, 1825. He appealed to
historical documents and the treatises of Catholic
writers to show that though the Catholic Church was
different from and less desirable than the Church of
England on the doctrines of Baptism, the Eucharist,
Penance, and Indulgences, it was nevertheless not as
idolatrous as Protestant critics had claimed. On the
subject of images, according to Lloyd, it "is and
always has been the unquestionable doctrine of the
Romish Church, that images are not to be
worshipped as God." Against the Protestant accusation that the adoration of the Virgin Mary and the
invocation of saints constituted idolatry, he argued

76. *Ibid.,* pp. 280-1, 283, 284.

that "in the public formularies of their church, and even in the belief and practice of the best informed among them, there is nothing of idolatry." Practical, popular idolatry was another matter: "the principles relating to the worship of the Virgin [are] calculated to lead, in the end, to positive idolatry; and we are well convinced, and we have strong grounds for our conviction, that a large portion of the lower classes are in this point guilty of it." Even in his most liberal treatment of Roman Catholicism, there was imbedded a constant streak of Protestant chauvinism: "Our full belief is that the Roman Catholics of the United Kingdom, from their long residence among Protestants, their disuse of processions and other Romish ceremonies, have been brought generally, and almost unknowingly, to a more spiritual religion and a purer faith."[77]

In November, 1825, Lloyd indicated that he was planning to contribute another article to *The British Critic,* on the political implications of Roman Catholic doctrine;[78] but he never got around to writing the article. He was simply too consumed with personal concerns and professional duties to put pen to paper on the Catholic question. With his brother, Edward, dying slowly and painfully in a Cheltenham hospital, he often left Ewelme on Saturday and stayed by the bedside until Tuesday, from November, 1825, until May, 1826.[79] "I have been distressed & harassed beyond measure," he confessed to Peel towards the end of the ordeal, "& have hardly been able to find spirits for the ordinary duties of

77. *British Critic,* 3rd ser., I (1825), 113-14, 148.

78. Lloyd to Peel, November 30, 1825, BM Add. MS. 40342, fol. 287.

79. Churton, *Memoir of Joshua Watson,* I, 285, 290.

life."[80] All the while he was busy with college matters, such as a disciplinary case involving an undergraduate who tried to appeal to the Dean to reverse
a verdict of dismissal by the regular officers of the
college.[81] Nor did his university responsibilities
become any lighter. In 1825-26 he served as an
examiner for the newly-founded Ireland
Scholarship;[82] and he was advising Peel on the Oxford people best qualified to sit on a Royal Com-
mission for reporting on Scottish universities.[83]

Although these varied activities amounted to what
Lloyd himself referred to as "occupations *quae nunc
describere longum est,*" his preoccupation with the
public and private lectures was what really prevented him from contributing any further articles to *The
British Critic.* In November, 1825, he explained to
H.H. Norris his reluctance to commit himself to any
immediate literary project: "I am occupied during
term-time from morning to night, with hardly a moment's relaxation; and in the vacation I have still
much to do, many *lacunae* in my readings to be filled
up."[84] Norris could hardly push the matter further.
He well knew that within a few short years Lloyd
had gained a national reputation at Oxford, and was
rendering solid service to the cause of the Church.

Some of Lloyd's students, finishing their course of
study, were beginning to seize outstanding academic
and political posts, while others were filtering into

80. Lloyd to Peel, May 10, 1826, BM Add. MS. 40342, fol. 343.

81. Lloyd to J.W. Whittaker, June 24, 1825, Bodl. MS. Top. Oxon. d.
    314, fol. 71.

82. Bodl. MS. Univ. Archives, W.P. Pyx I, fol. 18b; cf. G.A. Denison,
    Notes of My Life, 1805-1878 (1878), p. 48.

83. Parker, *Peel,* I, 377.

84. Churton, *Memoir of Joshua Watson,* I, 280.

country parishes. Whenever they returned to Oxford to visit old friends or to vote on some issue affecting the University, they invariably returned to Lloyd's private lectures. "It is delightful," one former pupil wrote to Archdeacon Cambridge, "to see the old fellow standing once more with his back to the fire, delivering out oracles of wisdom, as he did of yore."[85]

85. *Ibid.*, p. 274.

V THE IMPORTANCE
OF KNOWING LLOYD

BY 1826 LLOYD WAS RECOGNIZED not only as an outstanding teacher of theology, but also as an influential patron whose favor was coveted. When the
bishopric of Calcutta became vacant in 1826, Henry
Hart Milman, the future Dean of St. Paul's, was
asked by Lloyd if he was interested in the appointment. Uninterested in Calcutta, Milman was
fascinated with Lloyd's power. "He is, I think, likely
to be behind the curtains upon the subject," Milman
wrote to his wife.[1] Nor was he mistaken. It was no

1. Milman, *Henry Hart Milman*, p. 106.

coincidence that Edward Burton, a Christ Church man and one of Lloyd's favorite pupils, was offered the preferment.[2] In the early years of the nineteenth century, when the important political, military, ecclesiastical, and educational posts were invariably filled with young men from Oxford or Cambridge, even the most obscure college tutor was important in the scheme of patronage. "Never forget that you *are now* daily and hourly forming that reputation upon which you must depend wholly for your success in life," the ambitious Mary Chinnery wrote in 1809 to her son, a pupil of Lloyd's. "You should aim at surprising Lloyd, and surprising his expectations of you, that you may *subjugate* his opinion, and be quite sure of his mentioning you always in such terms as will advance your views." The reason was obvious: "Indeed Lloyd will be one of the chief instruments in forming the opinion of the world as to your talents and abilities! If *he* does not think you a clever man, nobody else will be likely to do so."[3] Yet if Lloyd wielded some influence as a young private tutor in 1809, the power of patronage was all the more in his hands after he became Regius Professor of Divinity in 1822. The smallness and informality of his private classes allowed him to know his pupils personally. Quickly he discovered the bright, conscientious, promising students, and from that most prestigious divinity chair in the kingdom he heard of opportunities and was called upon to recommend young men to fill vacancies.

2. *The Oxford University and City Herald,* January 27, 1827.
3. Mary Chinnery to G.R. Chinnery, May 10, 1809, Ch. Ch. MS. xlvii, fol. 123.

Nothing pleased him more. Patronage was as
personally gratifying as it was traditional. If a person
recommended by Lloyd was accepted, it meant that
Lloyd's judgment itself was being appreciated. In
1813, after urging Peel to assist William Bode in obtaining a position in the Post Office, Lloyd wrote to
Peel thanking him "very sincerely for the exertions
you have been kind enough to make *in my behalf.*"[4]
The italics, fittingly, are Lloyd's own.

At its best the practice of patronage was the putting forward of able men whom one had come to
know intimately, beyond the artificial norms of examination marks and even, in some cases, beyond
the accidental factor of birth. At its worst, of course,
the system was mere favoritism or pure and simple
nepotism. Frederick Barnes, a large, red-faced,
rather deaf Canon and Sub-Dean of Christ Church,
was credited with a marvellously candid, if grotesque, statement on the subject: "I don't know what
we're coming to! I've given studentships to my sons,
and to my nephews, and to my nephews' children,
and there are no more of my family left. I shall have
to give them by merit one of these days!"[5] If Barnes'
admission was unusual, his attitude was nevertheless
common. But not with Lloyd. Shortly after his appointment as Regius Professor, he informed Peel
that he intended to bestow Studentships "solely and
exclusively to merit" rather than to family or
political connections.[6] Shortly thereafter he request-
ed Peel's assistance in placing a Mr. Turner's
credentials before Lord Liverpool in order to obtain

4. Lloyd to Peel, April 4, 1813, BM Add. MS. 40226, fol. 63.
5. Tuckwell, *Reminiscences of Oxford,* p. 134.
6. Lloyd to Peel, March 19, 1822, BM Add. MS. 40342, fols, 69-70.

some small living and a chaplaincy abroad for Turner. Fearing that the application would be ignored or rejected because Liverpool had "seldom given preferment to applications resting on the grounds of merit," Lloyd insisted that he was supporting Turner solely because he saw him to be "an industrious & conscientious man."[7] Merit was the key.

Yet merit, for Lloyd, had several faces. Often when he used the term he meant not mere proven talent, but personal qualities such as honesty, forthrightness, and tone of character — that "ethos" that the Tractarians later emphasized so heavily.[8] When a Canonry at Christ Church became vacant in 1825, Lloyd recommended Thomas Gaisford — a graduate of Christ Church who had been Regius Professor of Greek, without a college attachment, since 1812 — in these terms. According to Lloyd, Gaisford's personal character and principles, even more than his professional achievements, should be considered:

> It is not from any personal regard to Gaisfd, it is not from the high credit wch he has reflected on an office conferred on him 12 yrs. ago by the Crown, with only an honorary salary, it is not from his exceeding greatness as a scholar, that I am anxious to see him placed in Christ Church. These are abundant reasons for conferring on him some dignity, but have no particular reference to a *Canonry* of Ch: Ch: It is Gaisfd's character & principles wch points [sic] him out peculiarly for this station above every other. It is his high & immoveable integrity, his sturdy de-

7. Lloyd to Peel, November 29, 1822, BM Add. MS. 38195, fol. 136.
8. See W.J. Baker, "Hurrell Froude and the Reformers," *The Journal of Ecclesiastical History*, XXI (1970), 248-55.

termination to maintain everything that is good in
the old system & his willingness to admit whatever is
good in the new, it is his boldness & fearlessness in
delivering his opinions & acting on them that makes
me anxious to see him placed within the walls of the
University in a station of authority.[9]

Merit, in other words, had to do with an intangible
assessment of character, a quality of no little importance in Lloyd's scale of values.[10]

Consistent with his emphasis on merit rather than
unprincipled favoritism was Lloyd's willingness even
to put forward Oriel men ahead of Christ Church
graduates. In 1826 he successfully recommended
William Ralph Churton to serve as chaplain to the
Bishop of London.[11] Churton was a "favourite disciple" despite the fact that he was an Oriel man.[12]
Newman later noted that one aspect of Lloyd's
"vigorous-minded and generous" nature was his refusal to "put his Christ Church friends unduly
forward."[13] The judgment was not based on
hearsay: Newman himself barely missed being put
forward by Lloyd. One morning in 1826 he received
a characteristically curt note from the Regius
Professor: "Dear Newman, step in, please, for a moment." Puzzled, the young don ran the short distance from his rooms in Oriel to Canterbury Gate at
the back of Christ Church, past the library into the
Great Quadrangle, to Lloyd's house in the

9. Lloyd to Peel, March 23, 1825, BM Add. MS. 40342, fol. 229.
10. The Canonry, in fact, went to William Buckland, the geologist, of
    Corpus Christi College.
11. R.H. Froude to Robert Froude, May 16, 1826, Oratory MS.
12. Churton, *Memoir of Joshua Watson*, I, 316.
13. A. Mozley, *Letters and Correspondence of Newman*, I, 209.

southeastern corner of the Quad. As he opened the door, he was hit with a blunt question: "Newman, how old are you?" "Five-and-twenty," he replied, only to have Lloyd end the interview abruptly: "Get away, you boy; I don't want you." Having hardly seen Lloyd for the past two years, Newman was mystified. The next day he heard that R.W. Jelf, a Christ Church man, had been asked by Lloyd to go to Germany to serve as tutor to Prince George of Cumberland, the future King of Hanover who would have become King of Great Britain had Princess Victoria died. The only specific requirement which Lloyd placed on his appointee was one of age: he had to be twenty-seven.[14] Lloyd's eccentricity was not without its arbitrariness.

Thomas Mozley, who later told the story, noted what a difference Lloyd could have made to English history if he had not been so set on finding a man who was at least twenty-seven years of age. Newman might well have gone into government or international diplomacy. Certainly he would have learned German, a feat which A.P. Stanley insisted would have changed the entire course of English religious history.[15] On the other hand, Newman probably would not have gone to Germany even if he had been selected. He already had several private pupils at Oxford and had refused various attractive tutorships outside the University, including one with Lord Lansdowne.[16] Conjectures of hindsight aside, Lloyd's sending Jelf to Germany in 1826 did affect Newman indirectly. When Jelf, a tutor at Oriel, de-

14. T. Mozley, *Reminiscences of Oriel and the Oxford Movement*, I, 33-34.

15. Mrs. Humphrey Ward, *A Writer's Recollections*, 2 vols. (New York, 1918), I, 143.

16. Maisie Ward, *Young Mr. Newman* (1948), p. 112.

parted from England he was replaced by Newman, whose Oriel connection was to be of no small consequence.

Jelf's tutorship provides a good example of the heavy responsibility entailed in putting men forward. Ernest Augustus, the First Duke of Cumberland, had originally contacted the Bishop of London, William Howley, requesting a tutor for his son, Prince George. The Bishop had then turned to Lloyd for a recommendation, and probably never saw Jelf or at most had only a perfunctory interview. Yet when Jelf arrived in Berlin, the Duke of Cumberland — unaware that Jelf was hand-picked by Lloyd, not Howley — wrote to the Bishop: "I know no person is a better judge of all that is requisite in the character of a gentleman who is to undertake the education of a young nobleman and therefore I am fully at ease on that point, and his religious and political principles were secure I knew, he being chosen and recommended to me by you my dear Lord the known Support and great Upholder of our Church & Constitution."[17] Had Jelf failed to satisfy his royal employers, some blame would have fallen on Howley, but the real onus would have been on Lloyd.

17. Duke of Cumberland to William Howley, July (or August?) 12, 1826, Howley Papers, Lambeth MS. 1754, fols. 48-49.

Failure was not out of the question. Soon after Jelf arrived at the royal summer lodge near Schönhausen, he began writing to Lloyd describing the difficulties of his new situation. The day, beginning early and ending late, was consumed with teaching the Prince, indulging gaily in dinner parties, and reading to the Duke and Duchess in the evening — with very little free time for Jelf himself to read or study.[18] E.B. Pusey, studying in Germany and living near Schönhausen, also sent Lloyd reports of Jelf's frustrations. By February, 1827, the young tutor was fed up with the constant noise being made by Prince George's drums and the demands being made on him by the Duke to write letters, to digest and explain all the daily news from English papers, and still to read fiction aloud each evening. Primarily Jelf was upset over the impossibility of pursuing any serious theological study. "You will conceive," Pusey wrote to Lloyd on February 26, 1827, "that for a mind not very independent of circumstances, there remains but little leisure or spirit for regular study. He does not repine at his want of leisure; by accepting the situation, he tacitly made Theology a secondary object, and under the circumstances he cannot, as a man, decline what the Duke requests." Apparently Lloyd had earlier insisted to Jelf — as years before Cyril Jackson had demanded of Lloyd himself — that he continue working unremittingly at his theological studies. Herein lay the source of Jelf's anxiety. He felt, as Pusey put it, "that others cannot know the extent of these occupations, that they will anticipate more than he can

18. Liddon, *Pusey,* I, 96.

perform, and there is no depression, nor bitterness of heart, equal to that created by the constant consciousness of the expectations of those, who have bestowed time upon one, with the prospect of their final disappointment."[19] By April, 1827, Pusey was less oblique: Jelf, he informed Lloyd, was "harassed by the prospect of not being able to fulfill your expectations."[20]

All the while Lloyd was receiving letters from the Duke of Cumberland (who had learned that the Regius Professor, not the Bishop, had actually selected Jelf), congratulating him on his excellent choice of a tutor for Prince George. On March 30, 1827 Lloyd wrote to Jelf, urging his protégé "to throw Theology entirely out of his thoughts" in order to perform acceptably the duties for which he had been hired. It was lamentable that so much was being required of Jelf; "but," as Lloyd noted to Pusey, "the situation is of such importance both to himself & his pupil, that he must not allow himself to be disgusted with it."[21] Finally, after much trans-Channel correspondence, the message got through to Jelf. By November, 1827, Pusey could report that his friend was "most happily established" in his job, much esteemed by the Duke and Duchess, and much loved by the young prince.[22]

Lloyd was gratified to know that one of his young men had settled in and was happily performing the tasks to which he had been sent. He would have

19. Pusey to Lloyd, February 26, 1827, Pusey MS.

20. Pusey to Lloyd, April 22, 1827, Pusey MS. In Liddon, *Pusey*, I, 113, fragments of this letter are published, but the references to Jelf are omitted.

21. Lloyd to Pusey, March 30, 1827, Pusey MS.

22. Pusey to Salwey, November 23, 1827, Pusey MS.

been doubly pleased, had he lived longer, to see Jelf become a Canon of Christ Church in 1830, continue as tutor to Prince George until 1839, deliver the Bampton Lectures in 1844, and serve as the Principal of King's College, London, from 1844 to 1868. Certainly R.W. Jelf was one of those pupils to whom Noel Ellison referred — who found Lloyd to be a "directing and controlling friend" as well as an able professor.[23]

Edward Bouverie Pusey was another, more famous student at Oxford who profited from Lloyd's refusal to limit his activity to the professorial lectern. "In Lloyd's generous conception of his own office," as Canon Liddon suggested, "it was not merely his duty to teach theology, but to encourage and assist younger men who gave promise of theological excellence."[24] On a personal level, it would appear that the two men were irreconcilably different. Pusey, somewhat puritanical, shy, and sombre, had little of the personality of the ebullient Lloyd, who was frank and gregarious. While Lloyd was ordering venison and crates of dinner wine and port for his parties at Christ Church, Pusey was lamenting the luxury of turtle soup at Oriel and joining Newman in opposition to the serving of French wine at the Oriel high table.[25]

Still, in Pusey Lloyd detected the intensity as well as the ability for serious scholarship. Fittingly Hurrell Froude, who was thoroughly intimidated by Lloyd's encyclopaedic learning and long lists of readings for the private classes, felt that Pusey was "so

23. Noel Ellison, *Protestant Errors and Roman Catholic Truths* (1829), p. 210.
24. Liddon, *Pusey*, I, 94.
25. *Ibid.*, p. 93.

uncommonly learned" that it was "impossible to
keep pace with him."[26] Like Lloyd, Pusey was a
scholar who compensated for his lack of original
thinking with a willingness to work long, hard, and
thoroughly. Also like Lloyd, he disdained the reputation of originality while laying emphasis on the
authority of traditional doctrine. Newman observed
that Pusey "was a disciple of Lloyd's not of
Whately's," but shrewdly added that "perhaps it
may be said, not even of Lloyd's."[27] Pusey, in fact,
outstripped Lloyd in the breadth of his theological
interests and certainly in the weight of his writings.
But Newman failed to observe that Pusey became
different from and greater than his tutor because
Lloyd pushed him forward.

In 1825 he encouraged Pusey to go abroad to
study the German language and theology. Although
the Germans were known to be breaking new
ground in Biblical scholarship, hardly anyone at Oxford could even read the language. Early in his
career as a tutor at Christ Church, Lloyd himself attempted to learn German, but soon gave up.[28]
Teachers of the language were difficult to find.
When a native German tutor came to England hoping to find a livelihood teaching undergraduates, he
invariably almost starved from lack of work.[29] In
fact, a knowledge of German was considered suspect
at conservative Oxford. In the same year that Pusey

26. R.H. Froude to Robert Froude, April 19, 1826, Oratory MS.

27. Newman, *Autobiographical Writings*, p. 74.

28. G.R. Chinnery to Mary Chinnery, February 15, 1808, Ch. Ch. MS.
    xlii, fol. 92.

29. In 1805 a German by the name of Heger could gather only eight
    pupils from the entire University: G.R. Chinnery to Mary Chinnery,
    March 15, 1808, Ch. Ch. MS. xliii, fols. 55-56.

left for Germany, Connop Thirlwall noted that in Oxford "the knowledge of German subjected a divine to the same suspicion of heterodoxy which we know was attached some centuries back to the knowledge of Greek."[30] The issue, of course, was not language, but political and theological liberalism. Since Edward Tatham had consigned those "Jarman" critics to the bottom of the "Jarman Ocean" around the turn of the century, the intervening years had not seen the dispelling of such half-baked isolationist views at Oxford. Yet Lloyd, himself interested in but admittedly ignorant of German theology, called Pusey aside one day in the spring of 1825 and said to him, "I wish you would learn something about those German critics." Pusey later told H.P. Liddon that his life "turned on that hint of Lloyd's."[31]

Since 1823 Pusey had been corresponding with a friend in France who had become an agnostic, and in that prolonged correspondence he was confronted with his weakness in French and his total ignorance of German. In refutation of his friend's arguments, he could recommend only those German works which had been translated. Thus Lloyd's suggestion hit him like a thunderbolt. Why not master the German language, in order to read that theology and philosophy which remained *terra incognita* for most Englishmen? After a few lessons with a private tutor, Pusey decided that the only sensible thing to do was to go to Germany — despite the fact that a recent contributor to *The Quarterly Review* had attacked German universities as seed-beds of liberal

30. Friedrich Schleiermacher, *A Critical Essay on the Gospel of St. Luke*, trans. and introd. by Connop Thirlwall (1825), p. ix.

31. Liddon, *Pusey*, I, 72.

ideas and radical violence productive of anarchy.[32] "I sail this morning at 8," Pusey wrote to Richard Salwey in the early hours of June 5, 1825. "I am going to Göttingen to learn the language for divinity."[33]

He stayed in Germany for four months, dividing his time between Göttingen and Berlin. Seldom has such a short period of time effected such a dramatic alteration in the perspective of a man. Attending the lectures of Professor J.G. Eichhorn, an indefatigible worker and prodigious, wide-ranging author, Pusey was struck with "the vastness of the world of modern learning" and was confirmed in his supposition concerning "the standard of work which was necessary in order to explore it." On the other hand, the rationalistic air of Göttingen instilled in him an intense desire for positive doctrinal truth as taught by the Church through the ages, regardless of the changing fads of Biblical interpretation.

He saw that German critical scholarship, which would undoubtedly soon make its way into England, was having its most devastating effect on the Old Testament — discrediting the Mosaic authorship of the first five books, showing the miracles to be mythological, and generally casting doubt upon the place of divine governance and intervention. Shuddering at the prospect of such ideas ever gaining credence in Anglican circles, Pusey decided to devote his life primarily to the study and exposition of the Old Testament.[34] This decision was at the core of his later suggestion to a friend that his first trip to

32. *Quarterly Review*, XXIII (1820), 447.

33. Pusey to Salwey, June 5, 1825, Pusey MS.

34. Liddon, *Pusey*, I, 74, 77.

Germany "changed in great measure the plan of my life."[35]

When he returned to Oxford in mid-October, the practical implications of his new commitment became apparent. Originally he had intended to be ordained on Christmas Day, 1825, in order to assist Newman as a curate at St. Clement's Church. Now those plans were altered. "My visit to Germany has opened to me a new line of professional study," Pusey announced to Richard Salwey, "& tho' I know not whether it will be of any use to any one, yet it seemed to offer a chance, wh. did not appear to be to-be-neglected *[sic]*."[36] He decided to delay the taking of Orders.

Unfortunately his correspondence with Lloyd during the visit to Germany in 1825 has not survived. As soon as Pusey returned to England, however, he and Lloyd carried on lengthy discussions concerning the state of German scholarship and German attitudes towards the Church of England; and the significance of the experience for Pusey. Late in 1825 Lloyd urged him to put his German to good use by translating Hug's introduction to the New Testament (a refutation along historical lines of the German naturalistic school of criticism). Pusey began the translation, only to receive the word that a Cambridge scholar had almost completed an identical project. To Lloyd he wrote in June, 1826, that he was abandoning the work "with some regret."[37]

Actually the regret was not very great. During the past several months Lloyd had been urging Pusey to

35. Pusey to Salwey, November 23, 1827, Pusey MS.

36. Pusey to Salwey, n.d. [1825], Pusey MS. Printed incorrectly, but smoother, in Liddon, *Pusey,* I, 89.

37. Liddon, *Pusey,* I, 92.

return to Germany to study the Hebrew cognates, Arabic, Syriac, and Chaldee. All the while Pusey was receiving encouragement from one of his old German professors, Augustus Tholuck, to return, and already he had made up his mind that a second and longer visit to Germany was desirable. Yet he wavered, until Lloyd sat him down and enumerated the benefits of the plan. As Pusey's biographer put it, "but for Dr. Lloyd, the second, longer, and in every way more important visit would never in all probability have taken place."[38] On June 10, 1826, in the same letter in which Pusey informed Lloyd of the "untimely end" of the Hug translation, he announced that he would leave for Germany within the week. He then added a note of filial gratitude:

> It seems unnatural to close this letter, without attempting to express the gratitude for your many kindnesses which one has so often wished to do in vain *viva voce;* yet everything, but the mere expression that one is grateful looks forced. You then, I hope, who should know how much reason I have to be grateful, will, I trust believe how truly I am so.[39]

Before Pusey left for Germany, Lloyd asked him to gather information on the modern German commentators on St. Paul's epistles. Who were they? What were their respective merits? What was their reputation among the Germans themselves? These questions, posed by Lloyd to Pusey, reflect the insular ignorance of Oxford Biblical scholarship in the early years of the nineteenth century. Yet they also indicate that Lloyd, for one, was eager to remedy

38. *Ibid.,* p. 95.
39. Pusey to Lloyd, June 10, 1826, Pusey MS.

the situation.[40] For several months he heard nothing from Pusey, who was struggling with the multiple declensions of Arabic in the sultry heat of Berlin. Finally on August 29, 1826, Pusey wrote a long letter, informing Lloyd that the information on the modern German critics of St. Paul was difficult to obtain because of the "peculiar character" of the professors in Berlin: Schleiermacher was too independent,[41] Manheineke was too devoted to a modern school of philosophy to be concerned with the ideas of others, and the "orthodox" commentators merely referred to the interpretations of the Fathers or the Reformers. Although Mosheim, Baumgarten, Michaelis, Carpzof, Storr and Tholuck were held in high repute, German criticism — as Pusey saw it, rather unclearly — thus far turned largely on the Old Testament and the New Testament Gospels.[42]

From Lloyd Pusey sought advice concerning how long he should stay in Germany. His Syriac instructor having left Berlin, he was now giving himself entirely to Arabic studies. But he was unsure as to "what effect this exclusive occupation of language-learning might have on the mind." Furthermore he did not want to miss Lloyd's lectures on the Epistle to the Hebrews, scheduled to begin in the Michaelmas term at Oxford. Pusey wanted to know if those lectures would be given at a later date, and whether Lloyd thought he should now stick with

40. In November, 1826, Lloyd also asked Pusey to gather information on the Catechism of Justus Jonas and the test of the Augsburg Confession: Liddon, *Pusey*, I, 98. Pusey's replies are to be found in letters of November 13 and November 23, 1826: Pusey MS.

41. For another of Pusey's letters to Lloyd on Schleiermacher, see Liddon, *Pusey*, I, 82.

42. Pusey to Lloyd, August 29, 1826, Pusey MS.

Arabic studies. His tentative plan, if Lloyd thought it advisable, was to remain in Germany until early January, 1827.[43] Of course Lloyd wanted him to stay, and even insisted that he should remain in Germany beyond January if necessary for mastering the Hebrew cognates.[44] Easily persuaded, Pusey stayed until June, 1827.

But soon he had need of more advice from his mentor. In November 1826, he received a letter from Edward Hawkins and John Henry Newman, both now tutors at Oriel, urging him to accept a two-year classical tutorship at Oriel. Both correspondents had already conferred with Lloyd and had extracted — according to their interpretation — a vague consent to the effect that it would be "useful, or, at least, not unadvisable" for Pusey to accept the appointment. To Lloyd, however, Pusey protested that a classics tutor at Oriel had to lecture as well as supervise students privately, and that such an effort at the present time would constitute "a total interruption" of his Hebrew, Syriac, Chaldee, and Arabic studies. Such an interruption would possibly mean an abandonment of Old Testament studies altogether, for Pusey would lose the ground he had gained. He proposed an alternate scheme, and would make this "confined offer" to the fellows of Oriel. He would accept a theological rather than a classical tutorship, thus remaining in a field of study which would complement his work on Old Testament languages. Pusey then begged Lloyd's pardon for such a long letter. "But as I am understood (and indeed rightly) to value your opinion & advice more *than that of any one else,*" he added with emphasis, "if

43. *Ibid.;* Liddon, *Pusey,* I, 97-98.
44. Pusey to Lloyd, November 13, 1826, Pusey MS.

your opinion is given against me in this instance, it would of course much increase the difficulty of persisting in making this confined offer, tho' I feel that I cannot offer more without sacrificing the objects which I have most at heart."[45]

Although Lloyd offered no opposition to the plan, the fellows of Oriel were not agreeable to Pusey's proposal. They wanted a classics tutor, and decided to look elsewhere once they learned of Pusey's fixed mind.[46] So Pusey returned to his studies, putting in fourteen hours a day on Arabic. He had to work exceptionally hard, as he explained to Newman, because he had started relatively late. Whereas in England one did not begin to study Hebrew until one was at least twenty-two, in Germany Hebrew was universally begun at fourteen and Arabic usually followed within a year or two.[47] Pusey therefore found himself having to work even harder than the Germans. Lloyd, hearing of his rigorous schedule, warned him not to break his health, prompting Pusey to reply that though he had been laboring intensely, he was "not unwell, but [merely] fatigued." Unsatisfied with the answer, Lloyd wrote again "in all seriousness, and not, as heretofore, half in joke, half in earnest":

> You know me well enough to believe that I would not check you, if I did not think it necessary; but what advantage can it be, either to yourself or the world, that you should kill yourself with study? Besides, I cannot forget that I have a fearful degree of responsibility belonging to myself in this case, as I consider myself to have been, in a great degree, the cause of your German travels. What will your family

45. Pusey to Lloyd, November 23, 1826, Pusey MS.
46. Liddon, *Pusey*, I, 104.
47. *Ibid.*, p. 101.

think of *me*, if you should kill yourself with studying with your German professors?

So send me word that you are quite recovered, and that you do not propose making yourself ill again, and that you will not work more than half as hard as you have done hitherto.[48]

Pusey labored on until June, 1827, alternating Hebrew with Syriac and Arabic. By the time he left Germany he had accomplished his goal of equipping himself in the Semitic languages in order to be a first-rate Old Testament scholar. Furthermore, he had imbibed some of the method and dedication, if not the content, of German scholarship; and he had become familiar with German protestantism in a way that few Englishmen could understand. In Germany a mark was made on young Pusey which would never be erased. As an old man, he often responded simply to the mention of Charles Lloyd: "Lloyd sent me to Germany."[49]

Following Pusey's return to England in the summer of 1827, Lloyd's fatherly concern was more directly expressed. Pusey proposed to revise the authorized translation of the Old Testament, a plan to which Lloyd gave his "warmest encouragement."[50] But that work, like the earlier translation of

48. *Ibid.,* pp. 112-13.
49. *Ibid.,* pp. 94-95.
50. *Ibid.,* p. 117.

Hug's introduction to the New Testament, proved to be abortive. Still not having recovered his strength after his arduous schedule of study in Germany, Pusey had to abandon the project early in 1828. All the while his mind was being diverted to the need for a criticism of H.J. Rose's book, *The State of the Protestant Religion in Germany* (1825). In Germany when the book first appeared in translation, Pusey had heard the reactions from notable German theologians who were appalled at Rose's assertion that German theological rationalism bordered on unbelief because the Germans had not, like the Anglicans, retained episcopal control over doctrine since the Reformation.[51] As early as February, 1827, Pusey was considering a reply to Rose, and wrote to Lloyd that blatant mistakes rendered Rose's account of German theology "such as even in the worst times of Germany had no corresponding reality."[52] But in 1827 he had to leave the issue alone for the sake of his Arabic studies. Early in 1828, however, as he encountered difficulties in revising the authorized Old Testament, Pusey once again took up the subject of German protestantism.

Lloyd remained a staunch supporter. Pusey, according to Lloyd's reasoning, had been to Germany, learned the language, and studied German theology and history under native professors; Rose had not. How could Rose criticize theologians whom he could not read, or analyze a situation which he had never seen at first-hand? Here was a chance for Pusey to

51. See H.J. Rose, *The State of the Protestant Religion in Germany* (Cambridge, 1825), pp. 29-32. For a summary of the German critics of Rose, see Liddon, *Pusey*, I, 149-51.

52. Pusey to Lloyd, February 26, 1827, Pusey MS.

give immediate justification for his time in Germany, and to come out with his first published work.

The plan back-fired. Pusey's book, appearing in May, 1828, as *An Historical Enquiry into the Probable Causes of the Rationalist Character lately Predominant in the Theology of Germany,* was far better received in Germany than in England. It was, as one might expect, too Germanophile. Pusey praised Luther and the German pietists, thereby contradicting the standard view of Anglican High Churchmen. He took an optimistic position on contemporary German theology, even arguing that orthodoxy would profit from an encounter with rationalism; and he used phrases such as "the scientific spirit" and "a new era in theology" which to English ears smacked of German jargon. Worse still, as he tried to explain the emergence of German rationalism, he coined the term "orthodoxism" to denote the rigid and narrow Lutheran orthodoxy of the seventeenth century which turned away from the "living faith" of Luther himself.[53] To be sympathetic to the Germans was bad enough, but to appear to be attacking orthodoxy was unpardonable. Much later, after Pusey repudiated most of this first published work, he explained to a friend that by "orthodoxism" he meant that "dead orthodoxy" of the post-Reformation era, with no reference to the present. He had no doubt that people would understand him. "But they did not; and hence came the reports, I suppose, that I myself was lax in belief."[54] The impact of those reports proved difficult for the young Oxford

---

53. E.B. Pusey, *An Historical Enquiry into the Probable Causes of the Rationalist Character lately Predominant in the Theology of Germany* (1828), pp. x–xi, 51.

54. Liddon, *Pusey,* I, 154.

theologian to overcome. Probably he would never have succeeded in doing so if Lloyd had not been his advocate.

While Pusey was away in Germany in 1827, Lloyd had been consecrated as Bishop of Oxford; and now, on Trinity Sunday, June 1, 1828, he ordained Pusey as deacon. Although Pusey was disappointed with the superficiality of the examination, he characteristically looked upon his ordination as "one of the most solemn days" of his life. The return to the small Christ Church Cathedral where he had often worshipped as an undergraduate, coupled with the presence of Lloyd who had been the dominant influence in his development thus far, made Pusey reflect upon the meaning of his life. Had he the power of gazing into the future, he could have detected a fitting coincidence in his being ordained by Lloyd in the morning at Christ Church, then assisting Newman that same evening in the church of St. Mary the Virgin. On the following Sunday, shortly before he assisted Newman once again in a communion service at St. Mary's, he wrote to his fiancée: "The person whom I am going to assist is a very valued and dear friend, with whom I should most wish to be joined in this holy office."[55] Little could he foresee that they were to be joined in a far more profound way, as within a decade the terms "Newmanite" and "Puseyite" would become interchangeable.

Lloyd inadvertently made that union possible. Since early in 1827 Pusey had been engaged to be married. As marriage would necessitate his resigning his fellowship at Oriel, he decided to take a rural

55. *Ibid.*, p. 143.

parish after ordination. But when Lloyd heard of
the scheme, he strongly objected on the grounds
that Pusey needed to remain at Oxford in order to
pursue his Arabic and Hebrew studies at the
Bodleian. Dubious, Pusey accepted the advice. After
his marriage in June, 1828, he and his bride returned to Oxford following their honeymoon —
with no home and no income other than a small inheritance. Arriving back in Oxford on September
12, they were welcomed by Lloyd, who lodged them
temporarily in his own house at Christ Church.
Himself living with his family in the bishop's palace
at Cuddesdon, Lloyd reserved one of his rooms for
his study where he received pupils, and turned the
other rooms over to the Puseys until they found a
permanent place of residence.[56] Thus in the giving
of advice and in the making of arrangements Lloyd
kept Pusey at Oxford; and there Pusey resided for
the remaining fifty-four years of his life.

Yet Lloyd was not finished with arranging Pusey's
future. Within a fortnight after the Puseys returned
to Oxford, Alexander Nicoll, the Regius Professor of
Hebrew, died. Lloyd wrote immediately to Peel, noted the speculations at Oxford concerning Nicoll's
successor, mentioned several of the possible candidates, and added: "The only person in or out of
the University that is properly qualified for the office
of Hebrew Professor is Mr Pusey, a son of old Philip
Pusey. He has devoted himself entirely to the Orien-
tal tongues & is, as I imagine, very learned in
them."[57] Except for Lloyd's intervention, there is little doubt that Josiah Forshall, the Keeper of

56. *Ibid.*, pp. 123, 178-79.

57. Lloyd to Peel, September 26, 1828, BM Add. MS. 40343, fol. 288.

Western Manuscripts at the British Museum, would have been Nicoll's successor. Forshall applied personally to the Prime Minister and to the Archbishop of Canterbury, indicated his readiness to complete a catalogue of Arabic manuscripts which Nicoll had begun at the Bodleian, and offered even to prepare another catalogue of Hebrew and Syriac manuscripts.[58] He did not reckon on Lloyd's influence.

Lloyd shrewdly pursued the appointment for Pusey. On September 30 he wrote to the Prime Minister, the Duke of Wellington, offering his opinion of the best men available. If the Prime Minister wanted an orientalist, Pusey was the best choice; if he desired, instead, a theologian, then Edward Burton was undoubtedly the best at Oxford; or if he wished to have a half-orientalist and half-theologian, Nicolas Vansittart would do.[59] Immediately thereafter, however, Lloyd wrote to Peel urging him to push for an orientalist — Pusey, of course.[60]

On October 4 the Archbishop of Canterbury, William Howley, consulted Lloyd on the matter. Himself having been absent from the University for fifteen years, Howley did not know if there was any Oxford man who could do anything more than conjugate verbs with students beginning Hebrew. "If you can give information for or against any supposable applicants I shall of course receive it in confidence, having no other object than that of giving my opinion, if it should be required, in favour of the

58. Liddon, *Pusey*, I, 181.
59. Lloyd to Peel, September 30, 1828, BM Add. MS. 40343, fol. 290. Here Lloyd explained his letter to Wellington.
60. Lloyd to Peel, October 1, 1828, BM Add. MS. 40343, fol. 291.

fittest man."[61] After submitting Pusey's name to the Archbishop, Lloyd instructed Pusey himself to ask influential friends to write supporting letters of recommendation. By October 9 the rumor was circulating in Oxford common rooms that Pusey would be the next Regius Professor of Hebrew.[62]

Those rumors were premature. One of Pusey's friends informed him that some church dignitaries thought him "latitudinarian" as a result of his book on German protestantism. His sympathy for German theology and his apparent criticism of orthodoxy ("orthodoxism") had lost him support in High Church circles. Pusey, upset, wrote Lloyd a long letter detailing his views on the inspiration of the Scriptures, original sin, the procession of the Holy Spirit, prophecy, and the divinity of Christ.[63] Thus he began retracting his youthful liberal inclinations as expressed in the *Historical Enquiry* of 1828, a retraction which would culminate in a thoroughly conservative position in the 1830's.[64] Lloyd, pleased with Pusey's clarification, informed Peel that he was "now entirely satisfied" that Pusey's theological views were acceptable;[65] and he then sent a condensed version of Pusey's statement to Archbishop Howley.[66]

61. William Howley to Lloyd, October 4, 1828, Pusey MS. Thomas Gaisford was also concerned that apparently no able man was available at Oxford: Liddon, *Pusey,* I, 182.

62. John Keble to J.H. Newman, October 9, 1828, Keble College MS. 4.

63. Liddon, *Pusey,* I, 184-85.

64. See W.J. Baker, "Julius Charles Hare: A Victorian Interpreter of Luther," *The South Atlantic Quarterly,* LXX (1971), 97-98.

65. Lloyd to Peel, October 3, 1828, BM Add. MS. 40343, fol. 298.

66. Pusey to Lloyd, October, 1828, Pusey MS.

Apparently Howley was satisfied, as was the Duke of Wellington. On November 12 Wellington recommended Pusey to King George IV as one who was "strongly recommended by the Heads of the Church, and by all those capable of forming an opinion of the qualifications of the individual who ought to be appointed to fill that office."[67] Beneath the official verbiage the truth of the case lay submerged: Lloyd, who for the past five years had supervised Pusey's development, had now pulled all the strings necessary to place his young protégé in a chair of high repute. On the same day that Pusey received the offer from the Prime Minister, Lloyd received information at Cuddesdon that his efforts had been successful. Soon a carriage arrived in front of the Bishop's home, bringing the Puseys from Oxford. Happiness was shared, deferential gratitude was poured out from pupil to master, and Lloyd had a few gems of fatherly advice: Pusey should be careful not to offend his elder colleagues, nor to shake the faith of the simple-minded. Having come to his appointment under a cloud of suspicion, he should take heed not to arouse further suspicion. "Remember," Lloyd concluded, "you must be circumspect, you will be φθονερῶν φθονερώτατος," the most envied of the envious.[68]

Upon returning to Oxford in the evening, Pusey wrote a letter of acceptance to the Prime Minister. He made the curious mistake, however, of accepting the appointment "to the Regius Professorship of Divinity in this University." Canon Liddon, Pusey's

67. Liddon, *Pusey*, I, 186.
68. Tuckwell, *Reminiscences of Oxford*, p. 141.

official biographer, interpreted this slip of the pen as a subconscious expression of Pusey's conception of his role as being primarily theological rather then linguistic.[69] But another interpretation is equally plausible: Pusey's theological and academic development, as well as his now being placed in the Regius chair of Hebrew, was inseparably related to the guidance of the Regius Professor of Divinity. Charles Lloyd was a most important man behind the curtains for Pusey, as he was for so many others at Oxford in the 1820's.

69. Liddon, *Pusey*, I, 187-88.

VI   A BISHOP AND HIS TROUBLED SEE

EAGER AS HE WAS to further the cause of his students and friends, Lloyd never for a moment lost sight of his own interests. His magnanimity did not conflict with his ambition. Occasionally the ambition soared, as in 1824 when he envisaged himself as a successor to C.H. Hall as Dean of Christ Church, and informed Peel that if Lord Liverpool should inquire, "I send you word that, *tho' I will not ask for it I shall accept it, if it be offered me.*"[1] Sending Peel a long exposition of his own qualifications for the Deanery,

1. Lloyd to Peel, January 18, 1824, BM Add. MS. 40342, fol. 125.

Lloyd claimed that Cyril Jackson had long ago told him that one day he should be Dean; then he added that if he was placed in the Deanery he would "take care that Christ Church shall hold up her head."[2]

Despite his good intentions, Lloyd's prospects for the Deanery were not strong. His age (40) was no barrier, for the last four Deans had been between 36 and 48 years of age when appointed. Since 1689, however, the vast majority of Deans had not only been Old Westminsters but also experienced Censors and Canons of Christ Church. From Eton, Lloyd had held the office of Censor for a mere four months in 1819, and had been a Canon for only two years. Peter Elmsley, the Camden Professor of Ancient History and one of the most distinguished Old Westminsters of the day, informed Lord Grenville that Samuel Smith and Edmund Goodenough were the only two possible candidates. He was probably right, though he admitted that neither man seemed "quite the *beau ideal* of a dean." Both were from Westminster; Goodenough, a former tutor and Censor at Christ Church, was now Headmaster of Westminster. Smith had served as tutor and Censor in the 1790's, had been a Canon of Christ Church (though not a professorial one) since 1807, and had held in turn the important offices of Sub-Dean and Treasurer. He appeared to Elmsley as "not quite so great a clerk as could be wished," but "the feeling both of the college and of the university" was "decidedly in his favour."[3]

Unable to ignore such opinion, Lord Liverpool appointed Smith to the Deanery. The tradition of

2. Lloyd to Peel, January 27, 1824, BM Add. MS. 40342, fols. 131-32.

3. Peter Elmsley to W. W. Grenville, January 31, 1824, Dropmore Papers, BM Add. MS. 59418, fol. 100.

selecting Old Westminsters thus remained intact until the appointment of Thomas Gaisford in 1831. Smith's tenure was, in fact, undistinguished: Lloyd probably would have made a better Dean. The multifarious duties of the office, however, would certainly have diverted his energies away from his theological studies and teaching. His immediate future lay in continuing his work as Regius Professor, and in looking elsewhere for the fulfillment of his aspirations.

A bishopric was an obvious possibility. But not just any bishopric. Only the See of Oxford would allow Lloyd to retain his Regius chair and thus complete his designs for a new school of theology at Oxford. On this matter Lloyd and Peel were in full agreement. Early in 1826, when it appeared that the present Bishop of Oxford, Edward Legge, would soon be offered the richer bishopric of Durham, Peel immediately wrote to Lord Liverpool suggesting Lloyd if the Oxford vacancy occurred.[4] Flattered by Peel's spontaneous recommendation, Lloyd nevertheless urged his friend to lift the appeal out of the realm of personal patronage to the "higher ground" of merit. Edward Copleston, after all, was being spoken of as a candidate for the Oxford bishopric, and Copleston was supported by George Canning, the Foreign Secretary in Liverpool's administration. Unabashed, Lloyd compared himself to Copleston: they were equals in scholarship, though perhaps Copleston was slightly superior in general knowledge; but on the basis of professional claims, Lloyd considered himself as high above his rival "as the Andes to a molehill." On the question of their relative influence within the

---

4. Lloyd to Peel, February 23, 1826, BM Add. MS. 40342, fol. 324. Peel to Lloyd, February 22, 1826, BM Add. MS. 40342, fols. 322-23.

University, he would give Copleston "a month's start
and beat him easily on any question that comes
before us." Throughout the entire Church of
England, Lloyd added, his own appointment would
be a popular one, while Copleston's would be quite
the contrary.[5] When his own career was at stake,
Lloyd was seldom given to understatement.
For the time being, however, the See of Oxford
was not available. Van Mildert, rather than Legge,
was translated to Durham. Yet Lloyd's appetite had
been whetted. When C.R. Sumner succeeded Van
Mildert at Llandaff, Lloyd wrote candidly to Peel:
"When the King thinks fit to send him to something
greater, you may place me where he is. I would as
soon have his preferment as any in England. A small
Bishopric and a rich Deanery form an union not to
be despised."[6] Momentarily at least, Lloyd shelved
his original insistence on the dual responsibility of
professor and bishop. Weary with "working day and
night" in fulfillment of his professorial duties,[7] he
was not averse to "retirement with good provision in
some easy Bishopric."[8] As several sees were changing hands in 1826, he was struck with panic at the
prospect of being forever ignored. Even
Peterborough, an unlikely choice, would be better
than nothing.[9]
Late in 1826, however, his attention was drawn
once again to the See of Oxford. Bishop Legge
became deathly ill and appeared to be "evidently go-

5. Lloyd to Peel, February 28, 1826, BM Add. MS. 40342, fol. 328.

6. Lloyd to Peel, March 26, 1826, BM Add. MS. 40342, fol. 335.

7. Lloyd to Peel, February 23, 1826, BM Add. MS. 40342, fol. 328.

8. Lloyd to Peel, February 28, 1826, BM Add. MS. 40342, fol. 329.

9. Lloyd to Peel, May 10, 1826, BM Add. MS. 40342, fol. 342. Some of
the above material can be found in Parker, *Peel,* I, 439-41.

ing," prompting Lloyd to write to several of his well-placed friends, including Peel.[10] In January, 1827, Peel again wrote to the Prime Minister, Lord Liverpool. Carefully referring to the principle of merit on which Liverpool had filled prior vacancies, Peel suggested a consideration of Lloyd's claims to the See of Oxford "so far only as such claims can be supported, by learning, and unwearied exertion in his Profession, by discretion, temperance and good sense." Lloyd had ably and energetically revived theological studies at the University, and if he was at all worthy of a bishopric, due consideration should be given to the "peculiar importance of enabling him to continue his present Divinity Lectures by the appointment to the particular Bishoprick which is so soon likely to be vacant."[11]

Liverpool was not easily convinced. Reminding Peel that Lloyd had risen rapidly and was probably too young (forty-two years of age) for a bishopric, he noted further that Robert Gray, a Prebendary at Durham, was being recommended by several ecclesiastical leaders, and even by the King himself. Yet Peel was not to be put off. In a somewhat curt reply he swore that he had never heard of Gray, "unless he be a clergyman who acted as a magistrate in the neighbourhood of Sutherland — of him certainly never as a candidate for the episcopal bench."[12] Lloyd, himself upset at the prospect of having his designs on Oxford thwarted, wrote to Peel that Gray was "the most absolute twaddle that the Church ever produced." Nor could he conceal a

10. Lloyd to Peel, December 1, 1826, BM Add. MS. 40342, fol. 381.
11. Peel to Lord Liverpool, January 18, 1827, Liverpool Papers, BM Add. MS. 38195, fols. 192-94.
12. Parker, *Peel*, I, 443-44.

bit of paranoia: "I told you some years ago that I did
not think Lord Liverpool over-well inclined to
me."[13]

Fortunately Peel remained calm. Convinced that it
was best "not to irritate an irritable temper by the
exhibition of any anger just now," he decided to let
the case rest for the moment.[14] He well knew that
with the petulant King George IV supporting Gray,
Liverpool was in a quandary. In early February,
1827, Liverpool was considering political pressures
and collecting ecclesiastical opinion on the matter.
Then an unexpected event resolved the dilemma:
George Pelham, Bishop of Lincoln, died on 7
February 1827, opening the way for Liverpool to
move John Kaye from Bristol to Lincoln, install Gray
in the relatively insignificant See of Bristol, and thus
be freed to deal with the bishopric of Oxford on its
own terms. The decision was sealed by William
Howley's reminder that though only Lloyd and
Copleston had any claims to the See of Oxford,
Copleston's theological opinions were unknown and
suspected to be on the liberal side. Lloyd was in by
default. Peel's suggestion that the appointment had
taken place "under circumstances most honorable
and satisfactory"[15] rings somewhat hollow.

Yet the event accurately reflected the ecclesiastical
and political temper of the times. Undramatic as a
whole, petty in its particulars, distinctly unheroic,
this was the way in which offices were secured in the
early years of the nineteenth century. If a man was
not well-born, as Lloyd was not, he had to be supported by the well-placed. Shrewd manipulations

13. Lloyd to Peel, January 30, 1827, BM Add. MS. 40343, fols. 15-16.

14. Parker, *Peel,* I, 445.

15. Peel to Lloyd, February 9, 1827, BM Add. MS. 40343, fols. 22

and calculated risks were forever part of the game. Lloyd himself was proud, as he wrote to Liverpool, "to receive my promotion from a Minister who, by the principle [of merit] on which he has distributed preferment at his disposal has, in my judgment, done more to rouse the energies and increase the character of the Church of England than any Minister since the time of the Restoration." [16] As a victor in the game of ecclesiastical preferment, Lloyd had cause to be magnanimous.

Shortly after receiving word of his nomination, he discovered that a substantial fine which had been lying dormant was awaiting the new Bishop of Oxford. Estimated to be in excess of £4000, it would more than cover the expenses of accession.[17] Lloyd, of course, was delighted. Only a year earlier, when he was setting his sights on the episcopal bench, he admitted to Peel that he did not want London or Canterbury because they were too big and busy. "But," he added, "I want money because I am poor & have children, and I desire character: for I cannot live without it."[18] He certainly got money, though relatively little compared to the other bishoprics in England. Added to his professorial stipend of £1500 would now be another £1500 from the See of Oxford — the lowest of all the twenty-six bishoprics except Llandaff.[19]

On Sunday, March 4, 1827, Lloyd was consecrated at Lambeth Palace by the Archbishop of Canterbury,

16. Lloyd to Lord Liverpool, February 12, 1827, BM Add. MS. 40343, fol. 30.

17. Lloyd to Peel, February 10, 1827, BM Add. MS. 40343, fol. 24.

18. Lloyd to Peel, February 28, 1826, BM Add. MS. 40342, fol. 329.

19. See Best, *Temporal Pillars*, p. 545.

Charles Manners-Sutton.[20] On the following Thursday he and John Kaye, the recently confirmed Bishop of Lincoln, appeared before Sir John Nicoll, Judge of the Court of Arches, to tender "their acceptation of the vacant Bishopricks and their assent to the election made by the Deans and Chapters of the two Cathedrals." They then proceeded to Bowchurch, read morning prayers, took the traditional oaths against heresy and simony, and received the official word that there were no objections voiced against their appointments.[21] In the spring of 1827 the Lloyds moved the short distance from the rectory at Ewelme to the Bishop's Palace at Cuddesdon.

One of the first duties facing the new Bishop of Oxford was the selection of a private chaplain. The decision was not difficult. "I am not only *happy* in being able to do this," Lloyd wrote to Edward Burton on February 17, " but marvellously *proud* of being able to give you your first step, little as I know that step to be — but it will derive some value in your eyes from the regard you bear me, and the pleasure I know you will feel in being able to be of service to me."[22] For several years Burton had been one of Lloyd's closest friends. Having come from

20. *Jackson's Oxford Journal*, March 10, 1827.

21. *The Oxford University and City Herald*, March 10, 1827.

22. Lloyd to Burton, February 17, 1827, Shrewsbury School MS. I, fol. 16.

Westminster School to Christ Church in 1812, he received a double first in mathematics and classics in
1815, went to the Continent after graduation to
work in the archives of Italy and France, and by
1823 had published three books. Following his marriage in 1825, Burton decided to forego the quiet-
ness of a rural parish in order to remain at Oxford
living on a small independent income, taking private
students, and pursuing serious theological study and
writing. In 1825 Lloyd recommended him as a contributor to *The British Critic* and urged him to produce an account of the doctrine of the divinity of
Christ in the period before the Council of Nicea.
The result was *The Testimonies of the Ante-Nicene
Fathers to the Divinity of Christ* (1826), a book with
which Lloyd was "mightily pleased."[23]

The selection of Burton as examining chaplain
was a fitting expression of Lloyd's embodiment of
the historic scholarly and ecclesiastical emphases associated with Oxford, as Lloyd himself performed
the dual role of Regius Professor of Divinity and
Bishop of Oxford. He continued to lecture as usual.
Within a week after he received official word of his
nomination, he felt the need to visit Lord Liverpool
personally but could not do so because of the public
lectures which were in session. With men "obliged to
come from all parts of the Kingdom for the purpose
of attending" the lectures, he could hardly afford to
be absent.[24] Frederick Oakeley noted that little
changed in the lectures except for the single addition of the bishop's wig, which hung on a peg on the
back of a door.[25] During the Lent Term in 1828 and

23. Churton, *Memoir of Joshua Watson*, I, 281, 284, 291-92.
24. Lloyd to Peel, February 15, 1827, BM Add. MS. 40343, fol. 33.
25. Quiller-Couch, *Reminiscences of Oxford Men*, p. 328.

1829 Lloyd delivered his lectures as usual, with no interruption allowed for his new ecclesiastical duties.[26] Nor did his interest in students and friends wane. "Lloyd is the new Bishop of Oxford," Newman wrote in his journal in 1827. "He is very kind, and takes great interest in my plan of reading the Fathers; but he says that our theological systems do not agree. They agree more than when I was in class with him, but I do not tell him so. I deeply feel his kindness."[27]

As Bishop of Oxford and Regius Professor of Divinity, Lloyd occasionally had a curious over-lapping of functions. For instance, when he or-dained young Oxford men, he continued to require the traditional note in the diocesan records attesting to the candidates' faithful attendance at the divinity lectures. The case of Richard Hurrell Froude is a good example. Ordained deacon by Lloyd in 1828, Froude had to produce a "faithful abstract" from the parish register of Dartington, Devon, as evidence of his baptism, and written testimony from the Provost and Fellows of Oriel College to the effect that Froude had "through the three years last past, lived piously, soberly, and honestly, and that he hath not, as far as we know and believe, written or main-tained anything contrary to the doctrine or discipline of the United Church of England and Ireland." But he also had to deposit in the diocesan records a note from Lloyd that Froude had faithfully attended the divinity lectures.[28] Then Lloyd, with the proper note from himself, ordained young Froude.

26. Lloyd to Burton, January 2, 1828, Shrewsbury School MS. I. fol. 34; *Jackson's Oxford Journal*, January 5 and January 26, 1828.

27. Newman, *Autobiographical Writings*, p. 210.

28. Bodl. MS. ODP c. 226: Ordination papers, 1828.

By 1827, of course, Lloyd's lectures had made him a prominent figure at Oxford. The episcopal garb merely made him more conspicuous, not always with the most satisfactory effect. "The new Bishop presented himself in his wig in church last Sunday," Newman wrote home on March 30, 1827. "He is much disfigured by it, and not known. People say he had it on hind part before."[29] Whatever the appearance, the new bishop was kept busy preaching sermons as well as delivering lectures, according to periodic notices in *Jackson's Oxford Journal* and notes in the private diaries of contemporaries. One of the most notable observers was the young W.E. Gladstone, who matriculated at Christ Church in 1828. At that time, Gladstone was wrestling with a vocational decision, as he was being strongly drawn towards a clerical career. Effusively he noted that Lloyd preached "a powerful Sermon" on August 10, 1828, preached "ably" on the following Sunday, and delivered "an excellent sermon" in January, 1829. [30] From a staunch Evangelical heritage, Gladstone still apparently did not chafe at Lloyd's orthodox High Church orientation. On September 7, 1828, he not only read *The Record*, a rabid Evangelical periodical, and sat all evening hunting cross-references in the Bible, in good Evangelical fashion, but also noted in his diary on the same day that Lloyd "preached an excellent sermon, in my poor opinion."[31] Although Lloyd had Gladstone to dinner and family parties several times,[32] he apparently never attempted to in-

29. A. Mozley, *Letters and Correspondence of Newman*, I, 163.

30. W.E. Gladstone, *The Gladstone Diaries, Vol. I: 1825-1832*, ed. M.R.D. Foot (Oxford, 1968), pp. 194, 196, 221.

31. *Ibid.*, p. 199.

32. *Ibid.*, pp. 195, 203, 222.

fluence his religious opinions.[33] Nor did he give
direction to Gladstone's clerical interests, else the
Victorian era might well have had another politic ecclesiastic rather than a religious prime minister.
While lecturing, preaching, and supervising
diocesan affairs, Lloyd continued to attend to
University matters such as examinations. In 1828 he
and the aged Martin Routh, President of Magdalen
College, cooperated in setting subjects for essays in
competition for a theological prize.[34] At the same
time Lloyd began altering the sytem whereby a student received his B.D. degree at Oxford. Before
1828 a candidate merely went to the Divinity Bedel
(an official concerned chiefly with processional activities) and purchased, for five shillings, a form of
logical disputation which had been repeatedly used.
Feeling that no real examination was involved in this
procedure, Lloyd proposed abolishing the entire exercise. He encountered opposition from the heads of
Oxford colleges, and compromised by replacing the
oral form of logical disputation with the requirement
of four essays to be written and then read aloud.
Unfortunately, as Burton later noted, this innova-
tion did not prevent the purchasing of material, but
merely made it more expensive. Whereas the old
degrees had cost only five shillings, the new essays
cost eight guineas.[35] Lloyd's piecemeal reform simply proved to be inadequate.

Yet the difficulties in setting straight the procedure for granting the B.D. degree were minuscule

33. John Morley, *The Life of William Ewart Gladstone*, 3 vols. (1903), I, 57.

34. Lloyd to Martin Routh, May 26 (1828?) and May 2, 1828, Magdalen
College MS. 487, fols. 24-25.

35. Edward Burton to the Vice-Chancellor of Oxford University,
January 28, 1830, Shrewsbury School MS., II, fol. 6.

compared to the diocesan problems facing the new Bishop of Oxford. Immediately upon moving into the Bishop's Palace at Cuddesdon in April, 1827, Lloyd was confronted with a fitting symbol of the dislocation of things. To his horror he discovered that a large collection of books belonging to the library of the See was missing. There was "not a vestige" remaining of twenty-four volumes of journals of the House of Lords, forty-four volumes of debates from the House of Commons, four volumes of parliamentary reports, a general index to the Commons' journals, two volumes of Domesday Book, and miscellaneous single volumes from several sets of books. Immediately Lloyd wrote to the late Bishop Legge's executor, demanding an explanation and restoration of the material. "These Journals," he noted in a characteristic vein, "are worth nothing to a private individual, they are only valuable when they are handed down regularly, and when, unless some irregularity takes place, they will always be complete. Will you have the goodness to make some enquiry about these Volumes?"[36] A reply arrived at Cuddesdon three weeks later. Those records and books had been sent off to Winchester by mistake, shortly after Legge's death; but they were "now, if not already at Oxford, on their way back."[37] Few of Lloyd's problems within the next two years would be solved so easily.

The diocese of Oxford, though small (Buckinghamshire and Berkshire not having yet been added to Oxfordshire), contained its full share of

36. Lloyd to R. Berens, April 27, 1827, Bodl. MS. ODP c. 663, fols. 16-17. All the following references to ODP are to c. 663 unless otherwise indicated.

37. R. Berens to Lloyd, May 16, 1827, Bodl. MS. ODP, fols. 18-19.

cases representative of the Church of England's state of disarray. Records were jumbled, information was sparse, vicarages were run down, curates were poorly paid and over-worked, priests were non-resident, and pluralism was rife. Lloyd had hardly moved to Cuddesdon before his secretary and diocesan registrar, Robert Morrell, recommended a survey of some episcopal property in the diocese: to value the Farms of the Bishop's tenants in order to make a fair allowance from the tithes due from them. In the same letter Morrell mentioned the scheduling of confirmations at Banbury and Ewelme, and added that no confirmations had been held in Banbury since June, 1823.[38] Evidence is not available to indicate how well Lloyd coped with the proposal concerning a property survey. Apparently he set up a schedule of annual confirmations. In July, 1828, he and Burton again traveled by coach to Banbury for confirmations. Lloyd wrote ahead to the vicar, asking him "to order beds for Mr. Burton and myself at Mrs. Norton's Inn," and agreed to accept the vicar's "hospitable offer of dinner on the 1st of July."[39] The new Bishop was beginning slowly to set his ecclesiastical house in order.

Before he could take effective action, however, he had to obtain accurate information on the state of parishes within the diocese. The collection of such information, which Professor Best suggests was "not the least of the branches of church reform" in the 1820's,[40] had not merely to do with patterns of non-residence, stipends of curates, or the physical condi-

38. Robert Morrell to Lloyd, April 23, 1827, Bodl. MS. ODP, fols. 14-15.

39. Lloyd to T.W. Lancaster, June 23, 1828, Bodl. MS. D.D. Par. Banbury, c. 11, fol. 31.

40. Best, *Temporal Pillars*, p. 198.

tion of buildings. Equally important were the opinions of parishioners, however accurate they might be, concerning the Church. On October 10, 1827, a young curate wrote to Lloyd from Asthall (near Burford):

> On my visiting the parish, there were no [Sunday] schools . . . I found the population consisted of peasantry chiefly but little removed from the condition of foresters. The others composed principally of Farmers, are dispersed over a considerable space, & they generally plead the want of pews in the Church as an excuse for their non-attendance. This complaint is by no means without reasons, & I have endeavoured to [make] further arrangements for their accommodation. My Vicar informs me that annual rents of £5 to £6 p. annum have been received for many years past by one of the Church Wardens, unaccounted for, and he believes wholly unappropriated.[41]

Although Lloyd was anxious to rectify such unseemly situations, doubtless he knew that Asthall's case of clerical lethargy, institutionalized deceit, and lay discontent was uncommon only in the sense that it was exposed so candidly.

In December, 1827, a far worse case was brought to Lloyd's attention. Shortly after a candidate for Holy Orders, Jackson Delman, failed miserably in his examination administered by Burton,[42] Lloyd received a letter from the Rev. John Stevens, vicar of Swalcliffe, who had taken on Delman as his curate. Stevens, old and virtually blind, offered to keep his curacy open until Delman was re-examined.[43] In the

41. John Wells to Lloyd, October 10, 1827, Bodl. Ms. ODP, fol. 100.
42. Burton to Lloyd, December, 1827, Bodl. MS. ODP, fol. 30.
43. John Stevens to Lloyd, December 27, 1827, Bodl. MS. ODP, fol. 31.

meantime, however, Lloyd had learned that Delman had already failed in an attempt to obtain ordination at the hands of the Bishop of Chichester. He informed Stevens that Delman's ignorance was "so gross" that it was highly "improbable that he should ever attain to the knowledge requisite for his admission to Holy Orders." Then he chided Stevens for his neglect in not having made those inquiries "which ought, surely, to be made before the appointment of any individual to so large a cure."[44]

On the surface it appears that Lloyd was being unnecessarily gruff to a poor old parish priest. But there was more here than met the eye. While Lloyd and Burton were first considering Delman's examination papers, an anonymous letter arrived from Swalcliffe revealing a remarkable case of pluralism, non-residence, and general neglect. None other than John Stevens was the vicar under fire:

> The parishes of Swalcliffe, Sibford, Burdrop, Sibford Gower, Epwell, and Shutford, containing three churches and a very large population are all served by one clergyman wherefrom the services at each are obliged to be shamefully hurried over, and the duty at Shutford is always at one o'clock, an hour inconvenient to all the Parish who also never have the opportunity of hearing the morning service at all. Besides this the Rectory house at Swalcliffe is let to poor people and the prayers that there always used to be twice a week are now never performed though several of us much wish to go to Church on those days and to have a proper resident clergyman which always used to be, nor was the church at Shutford ever added to these till the present incumbent. From this neglect there are four or five methodist places

---

44. Lloyd to Stevens, December 31, 1827, Bodl. MS. ODP, fol. 32.

in the Parishes all within a few years and the interests of the Church are gradually falling into decay.

There can be no fault found with the clergyman who now does the duty with great solemnity and has drawn many people back to the Church but *it is said* that the Curacy is about to be sold for a title and this is the *third time within four years* that it is *believed* so to have been disposed (for the Rector [*sic*] though a rich man would sell himself if he could).

It is earnestly hoped that the Bishop will restore the accustomed duties to Swalcliffe, and cause the Clerygman to reside in the parish and also take it into his kind consideration whether a Church and Parish so large ought not to have two services on the Sunday and separate churches that ought never to have been united.[45]

Though he knew that such problems existed within the diocese, Lloyd was moved to respond to these specific, detailed complaints. As the living of Shutford was in the patronage of New College, he inquired into the amount of the stipend and learned that New College paid £40 *per annum*.[46] Then he turned to a solicitor in London for an interpretation of the ecclesiastical laws pertaining to pluralistic holdings and stipendiary arrangements, only to receive the unsurprising news that the law was vague but probably negative on the question of whether or not the vicar's income could be employed to support three curates instead of one.[47] The issue even reached the desk of Christopher Hodgson, a promi-

---

45. Anon. to Lloyd, December, 1827, Bodl. MS. ODP, fols. 24-25.

46. R. Barter to Lloyd, December 21, 1827, Bodl. MS. ODP, fol. 26.

47. John Burder to Lloyd, December 26, 1827, Bodl. MS. ODP, fol. 27.

nent official in Queen Anne's Bounty, who agreed
with the negative ruling.[48]

The more Lloyd learned of the history of the
Swalcliffe and Shutford situation, the more depress-
ingly complex the problem appeared to be. Burdrop
and Sibford Gower, two hamlets within the parish of
Swalcliffe, had no churches though they contained
the chief population of the parish. Twenty years
earlier (1808), when Stevens was presented to the
living of Swalcliffe and Epwell, a Mr. Townsend
served as a curate to the neighboring Shutford.
Shortly thereafter, however, Townsend moved away,
and Stevens took Shutford and served all three
churches despite his chronic illness and gradual loss
of sight. For four years he recited the prayers and
liturgy from memory, unable to see the printed
page. Then he retired to London with his wife and
ten children. With vicarage lands totaling 182 acres
attached to the living, contributing to an income of
over £300, Stevens leased the land to a tenant
farmer and paid a curate a nominal fee to do all the
parish work. Now within the past year alone no less
than three unlicensed curates had come and departed immediately, dissatisfied with the heavy work and
low pay.[49]

Sympathetic to Stevens' physical debility, Lloyd
was nevertheless appalled at the neglect of the

48. Christopher Hodgson to John Burder, December 31, 1827, Bodl.
    MS. ODP, fol. 29. For a summary of Hodgson's work as secretary
    and treasurer of Queen Anne's Bounty, see Best, *Temporal Pillars*,
    pp. 225-30.

49. Stevens to Lloyd, January 4, 1828, Bodl. MS. ODP, fol. 37; Lloyd to
    Stevens, May 18, 1828, Bodl. MS. ODP, fol. 86. These problems of
    pluralism and non-residence were common in the Oxfordshire
    diocese: See Diana McClatchey, *Oxfordshire Clergy 1777-1869: A
    Study of the Established Church and of the Role of its Clergy in Local
    Society*, (Oxford, 1960), pp. 30-69.

parishes. "I consider it my duty," he wrote to the Warden of New College, "to exert whatever powers I may possess for the improvement of the place."[50] He insisted that Stevens employ not one, but two curates — one for Swalcliffe and Epwell, another for Shutford. It was not unreasonable, he argued, for a man making £300 *per annum* to pay £75 for a curate at Swalcliffe, and to relinquish the £40 that New College was already paying for Shutford.[51] But Lloyd did not reckon on the tenacity of his aged vicar. "It would be a matter of great hardship to me as an old incumbent," Stevens insisted, "laboring as I do under my infirmity and surrounded by a numerous family to be required to appoint two curates upon so small a vicarage for the purpose of performing three single duties in one and the same Parish where six miles would be the utmost to travel in the course of the day." The new Residence Act (57 George III c. 99) made sixteen miles the admissible range; and in any case, Stevens reminded his bishop, "most if not all the neighboring clergy have two and in most instances three services on a Sunday."[52]

Lloyd was not to be evaded so easily. He noted that the new Residence Act of 1817 also gave bishops "the power of remedying the evil" of clerical indolence; "& it ought to be remedied," he added, "for it cannot be considered as a light obstacle to the spiritual improvement of a Parish that the Service shd. be fixed constantly and regularly at the hour wch all men know to be the ordinary dinner-hour of the poorer classes, & also independently of this

50. Lloyd to P.N. Shuttleworth, January 11, 1828, Bodl. MS. ODP, fols. 39-40.

51. Lloyd to Stevens, January 16, 1828, Bodl. MS. ODP, fols. 41, 47.

52. Stevens to Lloyd, January 17, 1828, Bodl. MS. ODP, fol. 45.

serious inconvenience, that the Parishioners shd. never have the opportunity of hearing the Litany or Communion-Service in their own Church." If sympathy was to be a factor in the case, Lloyd saw the needs of several hundred villagers to be more important than the selfish interests of an incumbent, old and blind though he was.[53]

Yet Stevens continued to procrastinate, still regularly mentioning the possibility of having Jackson Delman as his curate if Lloyd and Burton would examine him again. By late January, 1828, Lloyd was so thoroughly annoyed that he commanded Stevens to come to Cuddesdon for a conference. Apparently a compromise was reached: Stevens dropped his insistence on having Delman as a curate and Lloyd backed down from his demand that Stevens employ two curates. In early March William Boyle, a young man from London, was employed by Stevens for £80 *per annum* to serve as the curate to the three churches of Swalcliffe, Epwell, and Shutford. The controversy appeared to have ended not with a bang but a whimper.

But not so. Boyle, like the curates who had preceded him, found the duties too heavy and the pay too little even to afford a horse which he needed to meet his Sunday schedule.[54] Moreover, Stevens had deceived him from the outset, assuring him that two of the three churches were mere "chapels of ease" attached to the nearby "mother church."[55] After his first Sunday in the parish, Boyle protested to his vicar, only to be told that he could withdraw from

53. Lloyd to Stevens, January 21, 1828, Bodl. MS. ODP, fol. 47.

54. William Boyle to Stevens, March 21, 1828, Bodl. MS. ODP, fol. 54.

55. Boyle to Lloyd, March 25, 1828, Bodl. MS. ODP, fol. 60.

his contract if he wished[56] — hardly a feasible alternative in a market grossly over-supplied with young clerics in search of employment. Boyle turned to Lloyd for help.[57]

Understandably exasperated, Lloyd wrote to Stevens and reviewed the case in all its details over the past several months, noting that the real issue was the neglect of parishioners. Most upsetting to the people of Swalcliffe and Shutford was the constant change of curates. "It seemed to you a light thing," Lloyd wrote sharply to Stevens, ". . .to continue in the same course, and to appoint curates from month to month as might best suit your own convenience without any reference to the wish of your parishioners, the call of Duty or the discipline of the Church." Those three or four curates whose services Stevens had procured in the past two years, all unacceptable and unlicensed by the Bishop, had left regularly in quibbles over pounds and shillings. "These are not the terms or principles on which clergymen are to be treated," Lloyd concluded, "and I should hold myself guilty of very gross neglect, if I permitted this system to go on when the Law had given me the power of checking it."[58]

Yet Lloyd did, in effect, allow that system to remain intact. Throughout the summer of 1828 the case dragged on, as charges and counter-charges, threats and pleas, filled the mails. Finally in October Lloyd proposed to split the difference in Boyle's demand for an additional £20 per year and Stevens'

56. J. Wallis to Boyle, March 22, 1828, Bodl. MS. ODP, fol. 57.

57. Boyle to Lloyd, March 25, 1828, Bodl. MS. ODP, fol. 60; Boyle to Lloyd, March 31, 1828, Bod. MS. ODP, fol. 65.

58. Lloyd to Stevens, May 18, 1828, Bodl. MS. ODP, fols. 86-87.

refusal to pay anything extra.[59] Apparently both
parties agreed to another £10 for the curate, making
Boyle's salary £90 *per annum*. Lloyd had come down,
all things considered, on the side of his incumbent.[60]
There was no little justification for Boyle's later complaint that the Bishop supported Stevens "against
curate and parishioners."[61]

These uninspiring details of an obscure conflict in
Oxfordshire would be historically meaningless if
they did not serve to illustrate not only the tensions
confronting Bishop Charles Lloyd, but also the
lamentable state of the Church of England in the
early nineteenth century. John Stevens appears as a
caricature — a proto-Scrooge of the collar — only in
his eccentric exaggerations, not in his basic tendencies. He exemplified the type of cleric castigated
mercilessly by an anonymous critic in 1828:

> No man can be either loved or listened to, while
> there is a prejudice against the disinterestedness of
> his conduct, and while the wants and passions of
> men are in mutiny against his reproof and
> persuasions . . . Vain is the ministry of him who is at

59. Lloyd to Stevens, October 1, 1828, Bodl. MS. ODP, fols. 94-95.

60. Boyle himself was quick to point this out: Boyle to Lloyd, October
     10, 1828, Bodl. MS. ODP, fols. 96-97.

61. Boyle to Stevens, April 10, 1829, Bodl. MS. ODP, fols. 98-99. Lloyd's
     successor, Bishop Bagot, continued to have trouble with John
     Stevens: See McClatchey, *Oxfordshire Clergy*, pp. 78-79.

once the plaintiff and the priest, the prosecutor and the pastor, the guardian of the flock and the sharer in the fleece.[62]

John Stevens was merely one of many represen- tatives of the abuses at work in a church wherein less than one-half the incumbents were resident,[63] in a system in which clergymen held several livings but gave "much less than the wages of a day labourer for the subsistence of their curates."[64]

Lloyd himself left much to be desired in his hand- ling of the Swalcliffe case. Admittedly the organiza- tional machinery of the Church of England "was cumbersome and creaked," as Professor Chadwick suggests.[65] But Lloyd hardly bothered to apply oil and certainly did not replace broken parts until local parishioners and an exploited curate bombarded Cuddesdon with their letters of outrage. Lloyd ca- joled and threatened, but was overly hesitant to ex- ercise his authority in dealing with his greedy and stubborn incumbent. In the end, Boyle the curate suffered most. Trapped in a situation where the curacy ranks were over-crowded, he had dreadfully little bargaining power. Both he and his incumbent knew that the latter could turn to either of the uni- versities, or to populous London, and find a replace- ment before the sun set. Thus Boyle was "completely

---

62. Quoted from *An Essay on the Tithe System* (1828), in *The Quarterly Review*, XLII (1830), 109.

63. Owen Chadwick, *The Victorian Church*, part I (1966), p. 34. Ox- fordshire was even worse than the national average. By 1834 near- ly one-half of the Oxfordshire benefices had non-resident in- cumbents: McClatchey, *Oxfordshire Clergy*, p. 31.

64. Quoted in W.L. Mathieson, *English Church Reform, 1815-1840* (1923), pp. 22-23.

65. Chadwick, *Victorian Church*, p. 34.

in his parson's power"[66] as Lloyd persisted in evad-
ing his responsibility, granted by law, to require a
reasonable stipend.

Lloyd's inclination to avoid difficult issues even
caused some consternation within the University
community. In 1826 H.B. Bulteel, a fervent
Evangelical, took the curacy of St. Ebbe's and proceeded to upset members of the University with his
enthusiastic preaching and low-protestant
heterodoxy.[67] Extremely popular with undergraduates, Bulteel attracted such crowds that they
prevented the regular parishioners from attending
the services. In May, 1828, the churchwardens of St.
Ebbe's complained to Lloyd about their curate's an-
tics, and addressed a remonstrance to the Vice-
Chancellor and Heads of Houses urging them to
forbid undergraduates from attending. At the next
meeting of the Hebdomadal Board "many violent
things were said by several against Bulteel." Even
the Principal of St. Edmund Hall, the Evangelical
stronghold, considered Bulteel to be "an enthusiast
— heterodox — insane!"[68] A petition signed by 146
members of the University was addressed to Lloyd,
urging some disciplinary action.[69] But he apparently
did little, if anything.[70] Bulteel continued to rant,
and in 1831 turned to preaching in Dissenters' meet-
ing-houses and so vehemently attacked the Universi-

---

66. See Best, *Temporal Pillars,* p. 207.

67. See Ward, *Victorian Oxford,* pp. 75-76.

68. MS. Diary of John Hill, May 5, 1828, Bodl. MS. St. Edmund Hall
    67/6, fol. 115.

69. *Ibid.,* May 10, 1828, fol. 116.

70. Tuckwell erroneously credits Lloyd with suspending Bulteel's
    licence: *Reminiscences of Oxford,* p. 227.

ty officials that Lloyd's successor, Richard Bagot, revoked his licence.[71]

Although it is obvious that Lloyd's forte was not in
episcopal administration, it would be unfair as well
as misleading to apply the reformist standards of
later Victorian bishops to his work within the diocese
of Oxford from 1827 to 1829. Admittedly he was no
Charles Blomfield, Samuel Wilberforce, or Connop
Thirlwall. It is important to note, however, that the
difference does not lie in the simplistic accusation of
indifference or vested interest. Like all of his contemporaries on the episcopal bench, Lloyd was born
prior to the French Revolution.[72] Thus imbued with
a worldly cynicism towards any type of radical, sudden alteration, he was not given to assertive in-
trusion against the established pattern of authority
even in the lower echelons of the ecclesiastical order.
One clergyman remembered years later that as he
was going to his first parish, Lloyd counselled him:
"Don't turn a parish upside down, because you think
yourself an angel."[73] Himself never claiming to be an
angel, Lloyd certainly never relished the idea of
turning his diocese upside down — no matter how
bad it appeared to be right side up.

Predictably traditional and pragmatic, he once appointed a curate and supplemented a stipend at Ad-
derbury only when it became obvious that the old
arrangement would be "derogatory to the dignity of
the Church."[74] But if he was timid regarding innova-

71. Bodl. MS. ODP, d. 109, fol. 26.

72. See R.A. Soloway, *Prelates and People: Ecclesiastical Thought in England*
    1783-1852 (1969), pp. 5-6.

73. F.E. Paget to Robert Eden, January, 1879, Bagot Letters, Pusey MS.
    I am grateful to Dr. Piers Brendon, Cambridge, for this reference.

74. Jane Smith to Lloyd, August 23, 1828, Bodl. MS. ODP, fols. 111-12.

tion, he was forever alert to the prospect of using established channels to the best advantage. Frequently he called upon the governors of Queen Anne's Bounty for financial assistance in the restoration of churches and the construction of new vicarages. In one case, Forest Hill, he informed the vicar that the governors of Queen Anne's Bounty would pay £800 towards the expenses of a new vicarage once the building was completed.[75]

Lloyd's inaction during the Stevens and Bulteel controversies was not merely the result of innate conservatism. Throughout 1828 and 1829 his attention was divided between his professorial duties and the issues of parliamentary politics. The question of whether a curate should be paid £80 or £90 paled in significance beside the repeal of the Test and Corporation Act and Catholic Emancipation, issues which required that Lloyd cooperate with Peel in hammering out a policy for the ecclesiastical as well as political sphere.

75. Lloyd to J. Mavor, March 25, 1828, Bodl. MS. ODP, fol. 108.

VII   AT THE DAWN OF REFORM

The "one overwhelming question"[1] in England in the 1820's was the Catholic question, an issue which divided Cabinets, the universities, and the nation at large. As Lloyd put the matter to Peel in August, 1827, the question of Catholic relief was "mixed up with every thing we eat or drink or say or think."[2]

The Catholic issue was essentially a part of the larger Irish problem, rooted deep in English his-

1. Charles Arbuthnot, *The Correspondence of Charles Arbuthnot,* ed. Arthur Aspinall (1941), p. 110.
2. Lloyd to Peel, August 14, 1827, BM Add. MS. 40343, fol. 63.

tory.[3] In the distant past stood Tudor penalties and Restoration Test Acts, but the anti-Catholic Revolution Settlement formed the basis of legislation that still excluded Roman Catholics from political life, with Irish Catholics suffering the brunt. Although the harsh penal laws of 1692-1727 were annulled by 1800, Pitt's Act of Union in that year abolished the Irish Parliament on the vague promise that the old measures barring Catholics from the English Parliament and governmental offices would be revoked shortly. Yet Pitt's ministry fell in 1801 over the Catholic question, and a coalition cabinet, "All the Talents," fell in 1807 opposed by King George III and divided among themselves on the question of Catholic relief. From 1807 to 1829 the Catholic question was debated in four of the five elected Parliaments.[4]

The bulk of English opinion was decidedly anti-Catholic as well as anti-Irish. Certainly most Tories, and some Whigs, agreed with Peel's assertion in 1816 that it was the Catholic religion in Ireland which was operating as the chief "impediment rather than an aid to the ends of Civil Government."[5] The vast majority of the established clergy stood firmly against the Catholics. At a popular level, the attitude of Mrs. Arbuthnot was commonly held and freely expressed, that the Irish had not only proved

3. For the following, see G.I.T. Machin, *The Catholic Question in English Politics 1820 to 1830* (Oxford, 1964); Ursula Henriques, *Religious Toleration in England 1787-1883* (Toronto, 1961); and J.A. Reynolds, *The Catholic Emancipation Crisis in Ireland, 1823-1829* (New Haven, 1954).

4. Peel, *Memoirs*, I, 288.

5. Parker, *Peel*, I, 236.

themselves "altogether unworthy of political power," but that they were, in fact, "a horde of bigotted savages subject to a Popish tyranny."[6] Oxford, the small but important portion of England whose opinion Lloyd was forever eager to convey to Peel, was also staunchly set against the Catholic claims. In 1808 a debating society found it difficult to debate the Catholic question because all the members of the society were of the same negative opinion.[7] Old superstitions held sway even in the supposed citadel of reason. Recalling the Oxford martyrs of the sixteenth century, Cranmer, Ridley, and Latimer, one Oxford man in 1807 saw in the Catholic question a demand to restore those "institutions which our ancestors had purchased at the price of much blood and bitter persecution." Thus he stood opposed to "the manifest absurdity of giving to this sect that which would enable it to be mischievous again."[8]

While Oxford's college scouts, lowly bed-makers, and unthinking egg-women were opposed to Catholic emancipation on superstitious and ignorant grounds,[9] fellows and heads of houses were largely anti-catholic on the basis of traditional Tory principles — what Lloyd once called "the old good

6. Harriet Arbuthnot, *The Journal of Mrs. Arbuthnot 1820-1832*, eds. Francis Bamford and the Duke of Wellington, 2 vols. (1950), II, 183. On this "popular anti-Catholic feeling," see Machin, *Catholic Question in English Politics*, pp. 65-87.

7. G.R. Chinnery to Mary Chinnery, June 2, 1808, Ch. Ch. MS. xliv, fol. 7.

8. Clinton, *Literary Remains of Henry Fynes Clinton* (1854), p. 26.

9. Morley, *Life of Gladstone*, I, 53-54.

[Protestant Established Church] cause."[10] Since the civil wars of the seventeenth century Oxford had been solidly Tory, strong on Church and King. The nature of Oxford's conservatism was explained well by Lloyd in 1825, when he noted to Peel that though "the rubbish of some of our old prejudices" should be gradually cleared away, *"the essence of the old Oxford principles* should still remain inviolate — that no shuffling or trickery shd. be introduced among us, no condescendence *[sic]* to new opinions for the sake of popularity, no change of our ancient sentiments, or anct. institutions."[11]

Lloyd, on the other hand, had little in common with the rigid ultra-Tories, his occasional statement to the contrary notwithstanding. From his eclectic study of ancient philosophy he had learned that though truth is unchanging, its manifestation is forever in flux. To Aristotle he attributed his conviction that one's principles may remain the same while one's practice alters, that "the circumstances of time & place & manner with the other predicaments of action, constitute the tests by wch any practical *measure* is to be tried."[12] This chink in the Tory armor, though rationalized by Aristotelian philosophy, was born of political pressure. Soon the chink was to become a yawning chasm.

Like Peel, Lloyd was imbued with a strong sense of political realism. Once he candidly admitted that a major consideration in the position Peel should take in parliamentary debate was "the prospect of being

10. Lloyd to Peel, March 14, 1813, BM Add. MS. 40225, fol. 224.
11. Lloyd to Peel, March 23, 1825, BM Add. MS. 40342, fol. 229.
12. Lloyd to Peel, April 22, 1827, BM Add. MS. 40343, fol. 57.

victorious or being beaten."[13] Seeing no virtue in clinging to a position doomed to failure, he approached political questions — whether at Christ Church or Westminster — from an empirical rather than an ideological standard. Thus he urged Peel to dissociate himself from those ultra-Tories who were possessed of "an illiberal disposition to maintain every institution good or bad, and to concede nothing to the feelings of the times, or the wishes of the public." Did not history speak "with a voice too loud to be mistaken," that "moderation is the only course to be pursued"?[14]

Concerned for Peel's political prospects, Lloyd urged him in January, 1828, not to chafe at the presence of ultra-Tories in Wellington's newly-formed Cabinet, in which Peel was Home Secretary. The various Tory factions needed to be united; cooperation even with the older, inflexible colleagues was momentarily necessary in order to win the confidence of the younger, more energetic and liberal men, in whose support lay Peel's future. "I wish them, by personal contact with the Administration," Lloyd wrote to Peel on January 16,

> to know that you support the liberal side; & that you only stop when liberality is degenerating into licentiousness. There is a liberality consistent with a mixed form of Govt: there is another consistent only with a Democracy. I wish it to be known that you have the former, & only want the latter: and I feel exceedingly anxious that the young men of promise should know this & remain with you, so that they

13. Peel, *Memoirs,* I, p. 77.

14. Lloyd to Peel, January 16, 1828, BM Add. MS. 40343, fols. 110-11.

may be content to serve under you at a future time.[15]

The words were not lost on Peel, still a receptive pupil.

Although King George IV had stipulated to Wellington that Catholic Emancipation should not be considered by the new Cabinet, events in Ireland made the issue unavoidable. On January 13, 1828, mass meetings of the Catholic Association were held in about 1600 of the 2500 parishes in Ireland, in demand of political rights. Englishmen, whatever their bias, could not ignore the spectre of united Irish action. Lloyd himself noted to Peel three days after the meetings of the Catholic Association that "the Catholics must either be kept down by force, or the Question must be granted. And, would to heaven, we were well rid of it!" Still, Lloyd was hesitant, hopeful that the Irish would quieten. He advised Peel not to "form any determination in regard to your future conduct on this point just yet."[16]

A more immediate issue was Lord John Russell's motion for the repeal of the Test and Corporation Acts. Though ineffectual, the old statutes dating from the days of Charles II requiring political office-

15. *Ibid.* fol. 112.

16. *Ibid,* fol. 111; cf. Peel's reply: Parker, *Peel,* II, 31. For the larger picture of Irish pressure on English politics, see Reynolds, *Catholic Emancipation Crisis in Ireland,* pp. 136-60.

holders and corporation members to take the sacraments of the Church of England, remained on the statute books. Partially applying to Catholics, the discriminatory nature of the Acts was felt most keenly by Nonconformists. Legally if not practically, theirs was a second-class citizenship, with participation in civil matters dependent on religious affiliation. Lloyd conservatively but logically noted that it was "perfectly absurd" to consider the "total independence of civil affairs on religious opinion" in a state where there was a Church established and controlled by law. Thus he collected fourteen volumes of arguments against repeal in order to arm Peel with the core of the major points of opposition. Still the political realist, he suggested that Peel should consult the heads of the Anglican Church, such as the Archbishop of Canterbury and the Bishops of Durham and London, in order to have their support in whatever position he might take in his parliamentary debates.[17] "If we are to be beaten on the C. & T. Acts," he wrote to Peel on February 26, 1828, "the less that is said the better, and I hope at all events that you will not be committed to keep up any opposition year after year. My only wish was, that *at this moment* you should not be exposed to the charge of an unexpected liberality on the part of the clergy."[18]

On February 26 the House of Commons voted for the bill to go into committee. This, Peel felt, was decisive. But should opposition be rallied in the Lords? What — Peel asked Lloyd — was the sentiment at

17. Lloyd to Peel, February 10, 1828, BM Add. MS. 40343, fols. 140-41.
18. Lloyd to Peel, February 26, 1828, BM Add. MS. 40343, fol. 178.

Oxford?[19] The reply came in the next post: Oxford was indifferent, and would go along quietly with repeal. Lloyd himself was in favour of letting it pass, but urged Peel to stay out of the matter as much as possible in order to save face.[20] For several weeks the two men corresponded on the subject, with Lloyd holding out for some sort of declaration of Christian belief in place of the sacramental test.[21] The declaration, introduced by Peel and supported by the majority of bishops, was accepted after minor amendments.[22]

One of the more interesting results of this rather unedifying deliberation was Lloyd's candid analysis of the present state of the Church of England *vis-a-vis* the State. Convinced that a system of established religion necessarily implied superiority, he argued in proto-Tractarian fashion that the Church's attachment to the State had, in fact, put her in an inferior position in relation to Dissenters and liberal reformers. The legislature, he wrote to Peel in March, 1828,

> has placed the Church of England under so severe a cognizance, has passed such severe laws in relation to her exertion of such [spiritual] power, has so impeded & controlled the action even of the Ecclesiastical Courts that the spiritual power of the Church of England is not only virtually but positively taken away by direct acts of the Legislature. For how stands the law? The Church of England cannot meet now in any assembly for the purpose of discussing points of Doctrine, of denouncing Schism, of

19. Peel, *Memoirs,* I, pp. 68-72.
20. Lloyd to Peel, March 2, 1828, BM Add. MS. 40343, fols. 189-90.
21. Peel, *Memoirs,* I, 70- 99.
22. See Gash, *Mr. Secretary Peel,* pp. 464-65.

making rules of Discipline or for any other purpose
of the same kind. You abolished all this when you
did in fact abolish Convocation.[23] Nor can her
ministers expel a noxious member, excommunicate
or anything of the same kind. You force them at
the same time, without any reference to right or
conscience to baptize, bury, marry Dissenters . . .
The Legislature in fact say [sic] to the C. of E. 'So
long as we guarantee your property we will take to
ourselves the right of controlling your discipline &
of preventing you from exercising any spiritual
Power over your members.' It is a villainous argument, & as oppressive as it is mean.[24]

A High Church Tory was precariously situated in
1828. To Charles Lloyd his own predicament was
clear.

In all quarters men observed that the repeal of the
Test and Corporations Act was a prelude to Catholic
Emancipation.[25] To Lloyd, especially, "the signs of
the times" were becoming "more and more
manifest." In March, 1828, the annual Oxford petition against the Catholic claims revealed a growing
opposition to the discriminatory laws. Although the
Protestants still outnumbered the Catholics, 63 to
32, the gap had narrowed since the last petition.
More importantly, whereas earlier the opposition
had been confined to the younger masters of arts,
now several doctors and heads of houses were
openly favoring the repeal of the anti-Catholic
laws.[26] In June, 1828, Lloyd stood firmly convinced

23. Convocation, the Church of England's governing body, was sus-
    pended in 1717, and was not revived until 1852.

24. Lloyd to Peel, March 21, 1828, BM Add. MS. 40343, fols. 236-37.

25. See Machin, *Catholic Question in English Politics*, p. 115.

26. Lloyd to Peel, March 13, 1828, BM Add. MS. 40343, fol. 210.

that emancipation would soon be passed, and reminded Peel that it would be far better if Wellington's Tory government remained in office in order to make the legislation more protective of the
Church of England.[27]

The reminder was well-timed. As Peel and Wellington were discussing the political necessity of
emancipation, Peel once again was considering resignation from the Cabinet on the basis of his long-
standing commitment to the anti-Catholic cause.
Wellington, needing to hold his Cabinet as well as
his party together, cajoled, manipulated, and evaded
whenever possible. In a Lords' debate on June 10 he
aired the possibility of dealing with the Catholic
question by legislation, but insisted that he wanted to
do so calmly, without pressure from the Irish. If
"the agitators of Ireland would only leave the public
mind at rest," according to Wellington's vague promise, "it would then be possible to do something."[28]
The tentative suggestion was designed more to
placate his own followers than to raise the hopes of
the Irish.

But when Wellington voted once again with the
majority to postpone the Catholic question, Irish
leaders were finished with their patient tactics.
Within a month they found an opportunity to renew
their pressure on the government. With William
Vesey Fitzgerald, a Protestant landlord in the county
of Clare, having to stand for re-election when he
took a place in the Cabinet, Daniel O'Connell op-

27. Lloyd to Peel, June 15, 1828, BM Add. MS. 40343, fol. 284. This
attitude was common among moderate Tories: see C. Arbuthnot,
Correspondence, pp. 114-15.

28. *Hansard*, XIX (1828), 1292; cf. Lytton Strachey and Roger Fulford
(eds.). *The Greville Memoirs 1814-1860*, 8 vols. (1938), I, 212.

posed him and won a resounding victory at the polls on July 5. Though as a Catholic O'Connell could not take the oath of office, his victory was a crushing blow to the government's delaying tactics. In August Wellington drafted a memorandum to the King, proposing Catholic relief, and sent an outline of the measure to Peel. Secrecy was the word.[29]

Lloyd, like most of Wellington's supporters, was unaware of these negotiations. From his correspondence with Peel in the autumn of 1828 one would not know that the Catholic issue was even being discussed. More parochial concerns such as Oxford's vacant chair of Hebrew, the private education of Peel's children, and the structure of the newly-founded King's College, London, were the topics of discussion between the Home Secretary and the Regius Professor of Divinity.[30] Neither correspondent mentioned Ireland or the Catholic question.

On November 24, however, Peel informed Lloyd that the Prime Minister wanted to see him (Lloyd) sometime around mid-day on the following Thursday.[31] Knowing that the Lord Lieutenant of Ireland, Anglesey, was finding it increasingly difficult to govern Ireland to the satisfaction of Westminster,[32] Lloyd had little doubt that the subject of "a most confidential nature" meant Ireland. He arrived in London on the early morning of November 27, talked first with Peel and then conversed for two hours with Wellington.[33] Already the Prime Minister had conferred with William Howley, the new

29. For the nuances of these maneuvers, see Machin, *Catholic Question in English Politics*, pp. 121-25.

30. These letters are in BM Add. MS. 40343, fols. 286-320.

31. Peel to Lloyd, November 24, 1828, BM Add. MS. 40343, fol. 323.

32. See Gash, *Mr. Secretary Peel*, pp. 535-42.

Archbishop of Canterbury; Charles Blomfield, Bishop of London; C.R. Sumner, Bishop of Winchester; William Van Mildert, Bishop of Durham; John Kaye, Bishop of Lincoln; and John Bird Sumner, Bishop of Chester. In these men Wellington sought the support of the most powerful ecclesiastical seats in the kingdom. With Lloyd, on the other hand, he hoped to make a wedge in the stronghold of anti-popery sentiment, Oxford. More importantly, he knew of Lloyd's influence on Peel, no small matter in the light of the fact that Peel's scruples concerning his public commitment on the Catholic question might still lead him to withdraw from the government. If Wellington could convince Lloyd of his scheme for emancipation, he would gain an ally in holding Peel. "The Bishop of Oxford was Mr. Peel's tutor," the wise Mrs. Arbuthnot noted, "so that he is an important man to gain."[34]

Never having been superstitiously anti-Catholic, Lloyd responded affirmatively to Wellington's treatment of the Catholic problem from "an empirical rather than a dogmatic viewpoint."[35] His own previous opposition to Catholic Emancipation had been bred of a traditional but flexible Toryism, not emotional fear. Having come to see that some measure of Catholic relief was inevitable, he was relieved to find the issue being brought up by a Tory, even a non-Canningite, Cabinet. Following his conference with Wellington, he was convinced that "the Church cd not desire better protection"[36] than Wellington's

---

33. Lloyd to Peel, November 27, 1828, BM Add. MS. 40343, fol. 325.

34. H. Arbuthnot, *Journal*, II, 224.

35. Machin, *Catholic Question in English Politics,* pp. 111-12.

36. H. Arbuthnot, *Journal*, II, 224.

plan offered; and one suspects that he was flattered to be in on the early negotiations. There is little evidence to support the popular theory, later enunciated by G.V. Cox, that Lloyd merely "took lessons of his pupil [Peel]" on the subject of Catholic relief.[37]

In early December Lloyd took up temporary residence in London in order to consult regularly with Peel and Wellington. Those discussions, according to the memoirist Greville, were being held to arrange matters "so as to make Peel's acquiescence palatable to the Church and the Brunswickers [the anti-Catholic clubs], and perhaps to engage the Duke to modify his intended measures accordingly."[38] At the same time, Lloyd was meeting periodically with his ecclesiastical peers and reporting the proceedings to Peel. The bishops, he wrote on the first day of the new year, 1829, were "decidedly hostile" to all concessions and would not consent to Catholic Emancipation in any form. Anxieties for the well-being of the Established Church mingled with old anti-Catholic fears. Little attention was given to "the political part of the question," Lloyd noted to Peel, "and your individual position was not mentioned."[39]

Finally Peel acted decisively. For five months his resignation had been on the Prime Minister's desk, but on January 12, 1829, he indicated to Wellington that he was ready to stay in office and pursue the Catholic question to its end. He sent a memorandum of his views to Wellington, to be placed before the King, and on January 18 he sent Lloyd a résumé of

37. Cox, *Recollections of Oxford,* p. 119.

38. *Greville Memoirs,* I, 226.

39. Lloyd to Peel, January 1, 1829, BM Add. MS. 40343, fol. 327.

the memorandum.[40] The King's speech on February 5 set the stage for a tumultuous debate.

The tumult was not confined to London. During the month of February the centre of events shifted momentarily to Oxford. On January 31, Peel wrote to Samuel Smith, the Dean of Christ Church, announcing his changed position on the Catholic question, and suggesting that he would resign his seat if the University so desired. In hasty consultation Smith, Lloyd and Gaisford agreed that they could make no decision binding on the University; they advised Peel to write to the Vice-Chancellor. Unknown to Peel, on the very day he wrote to Smith an informal meeting of several Oxford dignitaries was held to consider making a united petition to Parliament against Catholic Emancipation. On February 2 that petition was amended and Convocation was called for February 5 in order to bring the petition before the heads of houses.[41]

Peel's letter to the Vice-Chancellor, announcing his changed position and offering his resignation, arrived on the same day that Convocation assembled to discuss the petition against the Catholic claims. In the business relating to the petition, the anti-Catholic sentiment carried by a vote of 164 to 48.

40. Peel to Lloyd, January 18, 1829, BM Add. MS. 40343, fols. 329-31.
41. Vice-Chancellor's Diary, Bodl. MS. Top. Oxf. d. 16, fol. 3.

Then Peel's letter was read to the group. As the assembly of learned and dignified men buzzed like a room of agitated bees, the Vice-Chancellor wisely dismissed Convocation without any formal discussion of Peel's message. On the following day the Hebdomadal Board met to discuss the matter in a quieter atmosphere.[42]

Within the month of February Peel's resignation was accepted, his supporters persuaded him to stand in a new election against an anti-Catholic opponent, and he was defeated by Sir Robert Inglis. The details of this election have been chronicled: Professor Gash treats the subject from Peel's perspective,[43] and Professor Ward deals with the election as a part of Oxford's history.[44] There is no need to repeat the story. Yet some details omitted by Gash and Ward are of interest in relation to Lloyd's place within the University and his connection with Peel. To be sure, Lloyd did not perform very admirably in this matter. He left Oxford in a fit of anxiety on the day that Peel's letter was to be placed before Convocation. Whereas heretofore he had calmly and accurately served notice to Peel on the state of opinion at Oxford, on February 8 he admitted forlornly that it was "now exceedingly difficult" for him to ascertain "the real feelings of the University."[45]

Lloyd's most serious failing lay in his indecisiveness. Had he urged Christ Church at the outset to stand behind Peel, there is little doubt that the op-

42. *Ibid.*, fols. 4-5.

43. Norman Gash, "Peel and the Oxford University Election of 1829," *Oxoniensia*, IV (1939), 162-73; cf. Gash, *Mr. Secretary Peel*, pp. 560-64.

44. Ward, *Victorian Oxford*, pp. 71-75.

45. Lloyd to Peel, February 8, 1829, BM Add. MS. 40343, fol. 351.

position would have been intimidated and muffled.
But he hesitated, perhaps taking Peel's apparent indifference too much at face value. The Christ
Church senior common room (of which Lloyd,
because he was a canon, was not a member) was initially unanimous in their support, but when Peel
wrote on February 10 that he would stand for re-
election only on the grounds that success would not
entail a fierce fight divisive of the University, Lloyd
over-reacted to the rumors of opposition and instructed the common room to cease their activities
on Peel's behalf. Thus it was left to Peel's friends
outside Christ Church to lead the crusade for his re-
election. Soon Christ Church itself was split when
the Protestant party shrewdly announced that their
candidate was Sir Robert Inglis, himself a Christ
Church man. Lloyd as much as anyone bore the
brunt of Greville's indictment: "There never was
anything so mismanaged as the whole affair of Oxford."[46]

In fairness to Lloyd, however, it should be noted
that he genuinely believed that Peel would emerge
victorious from the election. Unfortunately his op-
timism was misplaced. On February 13 he glowingly
hinted at the prospect of victory by reporting to Peel
that the supporters of Inglis were men of inconsequential stature. Apart from Martin Routh there was
not a name known outside the confines of the
University.[47] But there was more than met the eye in
Croker's complaint that the election was dangerously
"democratical." What Croker meant, as he explained, was that in placing his Oxford seat at the

46. *Greville Memoirs*, I, 260.
47. Lloyd to Peel, February 13, 1829, BM Add. MS. 40343, fol. 368.

disposal of his constituents, Peel was setting "a precedent dangerous to the independence of the House
of Commons."[48] The election was also "democratical" in the sense that lesser fellows and unknown country parsons had single votes which
counted for as much as the votes of the Dean of
Christ Church, the Warden of Merton, or the
Bishop of Oxford, Lloyd himself. Little did it matter
that Peel's supporters "everywhere styled themselves
the 'talent' of the university,"[49] or that Inglis' ad-
vocates were described by *The Times* as being distinguished "for nothing more than the obscurity of
their station, the mediocrity of their talents, and the
insignificance of their characters."[50] Before he saw
the final poll in *The Times,* Lloyd betrayed a solid
streak of academic unworldliness in his summary to
Edward Burton:

> My idea is that (speaking generally) we have on our
> side all the learning, and ability of Oxford — that
> every person who has appeared before the public
> either as an author, or in high station has been with
> us — always exepting Routh — but men of fourscore
> must, in this case, be put out of the question.[51] The
> country clergy have carried it; and with the feeling
> that agitates them at the present moment, no exer-
> tions could have been successful.[52]

True, but only half true. In fact the country clergy
never would have carried the election had not their

48. L.J. Jennings (ed.), *The Croker Papers. The Correspondence and Diaries
    of the Late Right Honourable John Wilson Croker,* 3 vols. (1884) II, 7.

49. A. Mozley, *Letters and Correspondence of Newman,* I, 203.

50. *The Times,* March 12, 1829.

51. Martin Routh was 73 years of age.

52. Lloyd to Burton, March 2, 1829, Shrewsbury School MS., I, fol. 74.

interest been sparked by the energetic and able efforts of Inglis' committee. From the time that Inglis' name was submitted to the Vice-Chancellor on February 14 until the day of the election (February 26), the "Protestants" met regularly, circulated petitions, and informed the country clergy of the importance of the election. "Every spare moment of this week occupied in answering letters on the subject of the Election," John Hill, the Vice-Principal of St. Edmund Hall, noted in his diary for February 16-21. With the election still a week away, he had "received 23 absolute promises for Sir. R.H. Inglis with 3 more who will come if they can."[53]

They came in droves, some from as far away as France.[54] Every hotel and inn in Oxford was crammed. Although lectures were cancelled and undergraduates were encouraged to leave Oxford in order to provide beds for returning college men,[55] enough undergraduates remained to crowd illegally into the Convocation House on the day of the election, to agitate and jeer.[56] Nor were the country parsons any more reserved. One observer noted that "the violence of the parsons was beyond belief, and far beyond decency; they made faces at and abused each other."[57] The scene was so outrageous that the rural clergy were publicly censured in both houses

---

53. Diary of John Hill, Bodl. MS. St. Edmund Hall, 67/7, fol. 34. At the election, St. Edmund Hall had 35 votes for Inglis and only 6 for Peel: *Ibid.*, fol. 36.

54. *Jackson's Oxford Journal*, March 7, 1829; Colchester, *Diary and Correspondence*, III, 602.

55. Diary of John Hill, Bodl. MS. St. Edmund Hall 67/7, fol. 35.

56. *Jackson's Oxford Journal*, February 28, 1829.

57. Edward Law, Lord Ellenborough, *A Political Diary, 1828-1830*, ed. Lord Colchester, 2 vols. (1881), I, 366; cf. Colchester, *Diary and Correspondence*, III, 602.

of Parliament, prompting Greville to predict, with
uncanny accuracy, "that very few years will elapse
before the Church will really be in danger. People
will grow tired of paying so dearly for so bad an article."[58]

Perhaps one should not take too seriously Ellenborough's alarm that those anti-Catholic parsons,
"flushed with triumph," would "return to their
parishes like fire-brands, and excite the whole country."[59] But the election certainly divided Oxford, college against college, friend against friend. Even
within colleges there were bitter arguments. Oriel
suffered badly, as the election served as an omen of
quarrels and bitterness to come.[60] Nor was Christ
Church free from factions. Defending his own activity, or lack of it, Lloyd invited Peel to "look at the
state of our chapter: the dean neutral but rather
against [you] than for; Dr. Hay a violent antagonist;
Dr. Woodcock neutral; Dr. Buckland and Pusey for;
Dr. Barnes and Pett doubtful."[61] Lloyd himself suffered the rejection of several friends and pupils. As
Keble, Newman, and Froude voted for Inglis, Newman wrote to a sister that "the Bishop of Oxford
— whom I wish to love and do love — will, I fear, be
much hurt with what I and others are doing."[62] Keble, who had long harbored a "great regard and
respect" for Lloyd,[63] wrote to Pusey two days before
the election: "I cannot be quite easy without asking

58. *Greville Memoirs*, I, 266.

59. Ellenborough, *Political Diary*, I, 366.

60. See Ward, *Victorian Oxford*, p. 75.

61. Lloyd to Peel, February 18, 1829, BM Add. MS. 40343, fol. 374.

62. A. Mozley, *Letters and Correspondence of Newman*, I, 201.

63. Coleridge, *Memoir of John Keble*, p. 152.

pardon of all Mr. Peel's friends, and especially
(through you) of the Bishop of Oxford, if anything
in which I have had a part may have given him a
moment's pain."[64] An election on such an emotional
issue as Catholic Emancipation, without the benefit
of a secret ballot, could hardly help but upset Oxford's tranquil facade.

Yet the Oxford election provided only a pyrrhic
victory for the anti-Catholics. While Peel turned to
the pocket borough of Westbury, in Wiltshire, the
Cabinet proceeded to refine the bill for Catholic relief on which it had been working since January.[65]
Still, Oxford Protestants were not to be denied one
final protestation. On the very day of Peel's "election" to Westbury, March 2, a petition bearing
several hundred names of Oxford graduates and undergraduates opposing further Catholic concessions
was presented to the House of Commons. At the
same time a counter-petition was seized and
destroyed by a proctor.[66] The latter event was cited
by Lloyd three weeks later, when a huge petition
from Cambridge undergraduates against the government's motion was presented to the House of
Lords by the Bishop of Bath and Wells. Objecting to
such forms of political involvement by undergraduates, Lloyd proposed to table the petition on
the basis of the dubious precedent of the Oxford
proctor.[67] Despite his recent failure in the Oxford
election, he was still game for political maneuvering.

64. Liddon, *Pusey*, I, 200.

65. For details of the bill, see Gash, *Mr. Secretary Peel*, pp. 550-55,
     565-66.

66. Cox, *Recollections of Oxford*, p. 118.

67. Liddon, *Pusey*, I, 201.

Following Peel's introduction of the Relief Bill in the House of Commons on March 10, the second reading was moved on March 17. On the same day Archbishop Howley, under pressure from some of his more ultra-Protestant bishops, summoned nine bishops to Lambeth in order to determine if there might be a chance of acting unanimously.[68] No agreement could be reached. One or two bishops urged sending a petition to the King, but the group finally dispersed without any action being taken. Lloyd, who was not present at the meeting, was summoned by Howley to deliver to the Prime Minister an account of the proceedings. Upon meeting Charles Greville (yet another graduate of Christ Church) three days later, as both were taking their morning stroll in a London park, Lloyd assured Greville that at least nine, and possibly ten, bishops would vote for Catholic Emancipation.[69]

Emotions ran high. Throughout March and April "scarcely anything," according to Cox, "was talked of in Oxford" except the Catholic bill.[70] The Brunswick Clubs continued their appeals, and a number of anti-Catholic newspapers abused Wellington and Peel mercilessly.[71] Lloyd himself received several letters castigating him for his soft position on the Catholic question.[72] Nerves were irritated, literally, to a fighting pitch. In a letter to *The Times*, The Earl of Winchelsea, a notable ultra-Tory, accused Wellington of calculated treachery in his plans to give the

68. Ellenborough, *Political Diary*, I, 396.
69. *Greville Memoirs*, I, 275, 277-78. At the third reading on April 10, ten bishops voted for the bill.
70. Cox, *Recollections of Oxford*, p. 119.
71. See Machin, *Catholic Question in English Politics*, pp. 154-55.
72. *Hansard*, XXI (1829), 83.

Catholics full political rights in order to introduce popery into every department of state. Wellington's demand of an apology was refused, leaving the military gentleman no recourse but a duel. The fiasco ended tamely when Wellington missed on his first shot and Winchelsea fired into the air.[73] It was this atmosphere of frayed nerves, with conservatives thinking their beloved constitution betrayed, which set the stage for Lloyd's being made the prime scapegoat of anti-Catholic fervor within ecclesiastical circles.

On March 31 the Relief Bill, having passed the House of Commons, received its first reading in the House of Lords. Only three months earlier Lord Colchester had predicted that Wellington's majority in the Lords would be no more than four,[74] but the sides had shifted. The ultra-Tories were pressed to the wall, and they knew it. Not only had some neutral peers come around to support the bill, but also several bishops had been converted to an acceptance of the Catholic claims. On the first day of April Peel showed his trump card to the Cabinet: the Bishop of Oxford was "ready to speak at any time, and wished to follow a violent Bishop."[75]

Lloyd got his wish. After Wellington's second reading of the bill, Archbishop Howley opposed it on the basis of his oath of office, the integrity of the constitution, and the conviction of his heart. Then rose the Archbishop of Armagh, Lord John George Beresford, whose family had for decades been con-

73. Colchester, *Diary and Correspondence*, III, 609; *Greville Memoirs*, I, 275-76; Sir Herbert Maxwell, *The Life of Wellington*, 2 vols. (Boston and London, 1899), II, 231-37.

74. Colchester, *Diary and Correspondence*, III, 599.

75. Ellenborough, *Political Diary*, II, 2.

sidered the staunchest of all the upholders of the
Protestant Ascendancy in Ireland. Concession, he
argued, would not placate the Irish Catholics.
Political representation would only be the tool of
Romish priests, themselves controlled by that
foreign potentate, the Pope, scheming to subvert the
Irish Protestant Church. The issue, according to
Beresford, was simple. To give the Catholics political
rights was to sacrifice Irish Protestantism on the
altar of Irish Catholicism.[76]

Lloyd's stage, bare as it was, was set. His speech
was prepared beforehand,[77] not in direct reference
to any of the points raised by Howley and Beresford.
Apparently only one line of Beresford's address
touched him at all, as the reference to "those who
were once opposers of this measure, but who are
now its supporters"[78] struck him to the quick. After
the customary introductory shuffling, he defended
his altered position on the basis of the "cogent
necessity" created by recent events. Aggressive Irish
politicians, anarchy in Ireland, prolonged indecision
on the part of Parliament, and "the progress of
public opinion" were driving forces of change. Most
important, to Lloyd, was "the course which has of
late years been taken by the talent and education of
the country." Apparently in the back of his mind
was the recent Oxford election, when he and Peel
agreed that the "talent" if not the numerical majority
supported Peel. Now he saw at the head of opposition to Catholic relief those peers who had "reached
that time of life when most men have seceded from

76. For Howley's and Beresford's speeches, see *Hansard,* XXI (1829).

77. For the following, see *Hansard,* XXI (1829), 75-92.

78. *Ibid.,* p. 67.

the busy scene of human life." The future was with
the young, the young were in favour of emancipation, thus change was inevitable if not immediate.
The validity of Lloyd's interesting assertion could be
determined only by a statistical analysis of the ages
of the pro-Catholics, but such data would be beside
the point here. Suffice it to say that he was not being
very tactful in thus addressing an aged body of
peers.

In describing the first part of Lloyd's speech as
"very indifferent," Ellenborough surely must have
missed the caustic implications.[79] And not without
reason: the House of Lords was packed and noisy.[80]
Not only had the peers turned out in unusually
large numbers for the debate, but also members of
the House of Commons filled the area around
the throne. Even the latter were out-numbered
by London citizens who had waited impatiently outside the House until the gates were opened at 5
p.m., then rushed in to find a place to observe and
listen. Greville noted sarcastically that the House was
"very full, particularly of women, every fool in London thinking it necessary to be there."[81] In a calmer
refrain, The Times reported that many ladies in their
broad-brimmed hats were present, and that the early proceedings "were in general rendered inaudible
by the buzz of conversation in the house, and by the
continued influx of strangers for some minutes."[82]

79. Ellenborough, Political Diary, II, 3.

80. This factor alone would make even Hansard, not known for verbatim
    reportage in this period, a less than trustworthy guide to the in-
    tricacies of the debate.

81. Greville Memoirs, I, 283; cf. The New Monthly Magazine and Literary
    Journal, XXVI, 2 (1829), 41-48.

82. The Times, April 3, 1829.

Lloyd wanted to make his position clear. He was not happy that the progress of educated public opinion had become uncontrollably destructive of the old order. But "with fear, and agony, and sorrow" he would trust Providence to bring order out of chaos. Certainly he would not entrust the welfare of the Church of England to those zealous anti-Catholics, the ultra-Tories and their supporters. He was too mindful of the past when the Church was once prostrated, not by the Papists, but by the Puritans who were highly-principled but impudent in their anti-Catholic enthusiasm. Then, turning to rebut those accusations that his position was a perfidious one, Lloyd got himself into deep and treacherous water.

In reply to the charge that he supported a political union with idolatry, Lloyd reminded the House that if the Old Testament example was to be followed, then England was under God's curse for pursuing commerce with India and China, not to mention her commercial intercourse with Catholic France, Italy, and Spain. In fact, the Old Testament did not apply to a modern state. Furthermore — and here Lloyd's close reasoning was missed by much of his audience, and occasionally even by Hansard — the Roman Catholics were not idolatrous. Still needing to show that his views were not new opinions "formed out of deference to his majesty's government, and from a base and paltry tergiversation," Lloyd cited the article which he had written in 1825, in which he showed that the principles, if not the practices, of Protestants and Catholics were virtually the same. The Romanists, he argued, may have tendencies towards, and aspects of, idolatry; but taken as a whole, Romanism was not idolatrous. Such nuances could only lead to misunderstanding.

Although Ellenborough saw the last half of the speech as "excellent"[83] and Greville noted that Lloyd spoke "very well," Greville had a more appropriate closing note: "the debate has been dull on the whole; the subject is exhausted."[84] Practically all that could be said on the subject had been said. In the end, Lloyd reminded the Peers that the question was not whether the Church in Ireland was in danger, but whether Catholic Emancipation would diminish or increase that danger. Rhetorically he concluded, according to Hansard, "posterity will say, that the peers of England, when they admitted the lay-members of the Catholic body into the communion of the Legislature, still it did not put God out of the question; but went about Sion and marked well her bulwarks, that they might tell them that came after. . ."

A reporter for *The Standard*, a zealously Protestant London newspaper, was not impressed with the rhetoric, nor did he seem to hear the bulk of the speech. He simply noted that Lloyd spoke "rather flippantly on the subject of idolatry, which ... is not very becoming in a bishop, even though he be a liberal one."[85] At the opposite extreme, a writer for *The Times* praised Lloyd and concluded that his

83. Ellenborough, *Political Diary*, II, 3.

84. *Greville Memoirs*, I, 283.

85. *The Standard*, April 4, 1829. Ironically *The Standard* was founded in 1827 at the instigation of Wellington and Peel, as a conservative Tory organ of opposition to the Canningites: H.R. Fox Bourne, *English Newspapers: Chapters in the History of Journalism*, 2 vols. (New York, 1966), II, 23.

speech in favor of emancipation had "ensured a lasting reputation to that Prelate. It was heard with the
most earnest attention, and will be read with no less
interest and approbation, though, in reading, the
manner of its delivery, which was most animated
and impressive, cannot be seen or felt."[86] In fact
most reports of the speech were garbled.[87] Van
Mildert, absent on the evening of April 2, stood on
April 3 to debate with Lloyd on several points
which, according to the accounts reaching Van
Mildert, had been made the night before. In short
order Lloyd dismissed the criticisms as matters of
misinformation rather than disagreement. Yet the
spectacle of a present and former Regius Professor
of Divinity squared off against each other prompted
the next speaker, the Duke of Sussex, to remark that
when such supposed authorities disagreed, each
man was "forced by an imperious and urgent
necessity" to think for himself.[88]

The second reading was carried by a majority of
105, and on April 7, the House heard the third reading of the bill. They also heard a debate between
Lloyd and the Earl of Eldon, an old warrior in the
ultra-Tory camp, on the question of whether or not
the Roman Catholic religion was idolatrous. Eldon
was simply out of his element, as Lloyd was joined by
the Lord Chancellor (Lyndhurst) and the Bishop of
Llandaff (Copleston) in exposing his inadequate
arguments. In the words of *The Morning Chronicle*,
they "all mawled [Eldon] most unmercifully, contradicting his facts and demolishing his reasonings

86. *The Times*, April 3, 1829.
87. The best summary was in *Jackson's Oxford Journal*, April 4, 1829.
88. *Hansard*, XXI (1829), 146-58.

so that he could bear it no longer."[89] As Lloyd himself put the case to Eldon in the debate, if any Oxford undergraduates were to reason in such fashion, it would be evident that "they had rejected logic from their studies."[90]

Although he won the argument, Lloyd set himself up for vicious attacks from controversialists more able than Lord Eldon. It was unfortunate that the whole debate became fixed on the recondite question of idolatry. Lloyd's admission that the Romanists were idolatrous in some of their practices but not idolators generally, coupled with his insistence that the Catholics practiced piety similar to Protestants but simply under different forms, was all the ammunition needed by the ultra-Protestant press. *The Christian Guardian,* an Evangelical periodical, lamented that so many of the prelates supported Catholic Emancipation, and noted "the special pleading by which one at least endeavoured to vindicate the Romanists generally from the charge of idolatry."[91] *The Standard,* true to form, was much more explicit and scathing: "such casuists" as Lloyd would probably even "acquit the worshipper of *Jove* and *Mercury* of idolatry if he worship not also *Apis* and *Anubis.*"[92]

On April 10 the Relief Bill was carried in the House of Lords by an overwhelming majority. Left with little choice, King George IV peevishly gave his royal assent on April 13, confiding to Lord Eldon

89. *The Morning Chronicle,* April 9, 1829.

90. *Hansard,* XXI (1929), 508.

91. *The Christian Guardian and Church of England Magazine,* XXI (1829), 200.

92. *The Standard,* April 8, 1829.

that he felt like a man "whose consent had been asked with a pistol pointed to his breast."[93] On the very day of the King's capitulation, *The Standard* compared Lloyd to Samuel Parker, a former Bishop of Oxford (1686-8), who was universally regarded as a time-server by his contemporaries because of his submission to the demands of James II to have Romanists admitted to Oxford.[94] Still *The Standard* was not done with Lloyd. On April 20 the editor quoted from a Belfast newspaper that a coalition would soon take place between opponents of the Protestant establishment. Then what would "the Bishop of Oxford and his *liberal* brethren" say, the editor of *The Standard* wanted to know. "Whenever the work commences, we recommend that those bishops who have, in the spirit of passive obedience, advocated the political exaltations of popery, be especially fleeced."[95]

Yet there was a sense of relief, among the opponents as well as the supporters of Catholic Emancipation, that the tedious, threadbare controversy was finished.[96] On April 16 Lloyd wrote to Burton that in London "the Catholic question seems as much forgotten as if it had never been." Only among the county clergy did Lloyd detect any lingering bitterness, prompting him to print a corrected version of his statements in the House of Lords.[97] Convinced that his speeches had "been

93. Twiss, *Life of Eldon* Philadelphia ed., 2 vols., II, 221.

94. *The Standard*, April 13, 1829.

95. *Ibid.*, April 20, 1829.

96. See Machin, *Catholic Question in English Politics,* p. 179.

97. Twenty-six copies were printed: Lloyd to Burton, April 27, 1829, Shrewsbury School MS., I, fol. 82. The only extant copy I have been able to locate is in the pamphlet collection at Pusey House, Oxford.

carelessly reported in the Papers, & misunderstood
by the Ultras" in order to persuade people that he
was "a concealed Papist," he added: "I care little for
their nonsense or abuse, but I do for the clergy."[98]
Despite his protestations to the contrary, however,
the public abuse hurt deeply. He suggested to the
editor of an Oxford newspaper that a paragraph
should be printed explaining that his article of 1825
in *The British Critic* showed his opinions not to be
newly-formed on the basis of mere expendiency.[99]
He was especially sensitive to the rejection of old
friends such as Van Mildert. Although Edward
Churton later suggested that Lloyd was only "led into an appearance of public conflict with Van
Mildert,"[100] Lloyd himself noted to Burton that the
Bishop of Durham "behaved very ill" towards him.
Fortunately we are spared the details.

The deepest cut of all came from the King. At a
levee in St. James's Palace on April 29, George IV
warmly received a long queue of peers and ecclesiastics, bowing in recognition as each person
passed.[101] To those lords who had distinguished
themselves in opposition to Catholic Emancipation,
he was particularly friendly. But to those bishops
who had supported the government, he turned his
back and refused to speak.[102] Lloyd was crushed.
Though he knew that the King was a sick and
crotchety old man, dying, this humiliation before so

98. Lloyd to Burton, April 16, 1829, Shrewsbury School MS., I, fol. 80.

99. Lloyd to Burton, n.d. (April, 1829), Shrewsbury School MS., I, fol.
    81.

100. Churton, *Memoir of Joshua Watson,* I, 293.

101. According to *The Morning Chronicle,* April 30, 1829, more than 1300
     persons were present.

102. Twiss, *Life of Eldon* , II, 223: *Greville Memoirs,* I, 290.

large an assembly came as an enormous shock. His Tory past having never prepared him for this sort of rejection, Lloyd could not respond as did Lord Grey, who simply swore that he would never attend another levee at the Palace.[103] The mantle of a supposed liberalism rested uncomfortably over the bishop's cloak. As Lloyd left the grounds that evening, a dark cloud of depression followed him home.

---

103. Sir Herbert Maxwell (ed.), *The Creevey Papers* (1923), p. 543.

VIII   LLOYD'S LEGACY

THE WEATHER IN APRIL AND MAY of 1829 mirrored
Lloyd's mood. Never could men remember such a
cold, damp spring. The sun refused to shine, corn
would not grow, few blossoms could be seen, and
even the daffodils cringed for shelter from the cold.
In the first week of May a hurricane blew in from
the Irish Sea, destroying chimneys, roofs and
haystacks in the West Country; one London reporter noted the "merciless perseverance" of the east
wind which had been blowing for six months.[1]

1. *The Monthly Magazine, or British Register of Literature, Sciences, and the
   Belles-Lettres,* new ser., VII (1829), 649; *The Times,* May 2, 1829.

Hoping to break the spell of melancholy under
which he struggled, Lloyd on May 2 attended the
anniversary dinner of the Royal Academy in
Somerset House. Present, in the words of *The Morning Chronicle*, was "a numerous assemblage of guests
of the first rank and talent," including the Lord
Mayor of London, the Lord Chief Justice of the
King's Bench, the Chancellor of the Exchequer, the
First Lord of the Admiralty, the First Lord of the
Treasury, several dukes, marquesses, and earls; and
the bishops of London, Durham, and Winchester, as
well as Oxford.[2] That august company momentarily
revived Lloyd's spirit, but unfortunately his table was
beside an open window through which a damp, cool
breeze was blowing. By the time the festivities were
concluded, he had developed a sniffle and a slight
wheeze in the chest.

His health had never been particularly good. Extant correspondence dating from 1808 to 1829 is
punctuated with broken engagements and re-
arranged schedules because Lloyd was "suffering
horribly" with "very bad" colds and states of "severe
indisposition."[3] Coupled with a chronic bronchial
problem was a tendency to be overweight, a condition which was not helped by excessive port and
little physical activity. "He took so little care of his
health by exercise," Newman wrote, "that I do not
wonder at his constitution giving way when attacked
suddenly and violently."[4] Soon the chest cold de-

2. *The Morning Chronicle,* May 4, 1829.
3. G.R. Chinnery to Mary Chinnery, February 18, 1808, Ch. Ch. MS.
    xlii, fol. 108; Lloyd to Martin Routh, n.d., Magdalen College MS.
    487, fol. 23; and MS. 545, fol. 51.
4. Mozley, *Letters and Correspondence of Newman,* I, 209. Occasionally
    Lloyd had dieted: Lloyd to Peel, May 28, 1818, BM Add. MS.

veloped into a heavy cough. Physically exhausted and emotionally drained by the political activities of the past several months, Lloyd was on the verge of pneumonia.

Two days after the affair at Somerset House, however, he was still his old self. Upon meeting James Milne Gaskell, who was going up to Oxford to matriculate at Christ Church, he offered him the temporary use of his bedroom and study until permanent accommodation could be arranged. The generosity was tinged with a characteristic touch of bluffness: Lloyd specifically instructed the fledgling undergraduate "not to have the use of anything else" in his rooms.[5]

Over-sensitive to the end, he was bothered by more than mere bronchial congestion. On May 11 he wrote to Burton:

> I am very ill and have the hooping [sic] cough in addition to other evils, but my greatest evil is fretting. I hear from several quarters that the speech in the Committee gave great offence, — the speech in which I attacked Lord Eldon — and that some of the clergy & yeomen have put about a report that the Bishop of Oxford had gone over — that is, to the Pope. Now as a ridiculous report like this is just the

---

40277, fol. 276. But apparently he kept up the tradition of the bishops of Oxford and the Regius professors of divinity: It was said of William Jackson, Bishop of Oxford from 1812 to 1815, that he fattened "like the larger breed of animals" and *"died* of the true English complaint of *living* too well" (Allardyce, *Charles Kirkpatrick Sharpe,* II, 140); and one of the reasons attributed to the death of Frodsham Hodson, Lloyd's immediate predecessor in the Regius chair, was "high living and neglect of exercise" (Cox, *Recollections of Oxford,* p. 194 n. 2).

5.   C.M. Gaskell (ed.), *An Eton Boy; being the Letters of James Milnes Gaskell from Eton and Oxford 1820-1830* (1939), p. 160.

thing for farmers, send me word if you have heard
of it, & tell me every report you have heard about
the superstitious and idolatrous part of the speech.
And ask me the questions to which it might be proper to give a public answer.

A postcript was no less revealing of Lloyd's frame of
mind: "Pray send me with what accuracy you can the
reports about the idolatrous part. I am very, very
anxious about it." Burton later scribbled a note on
the manuscript letter that "the Bishop was not in full
possession of his faculties, when he wrote this,"[6] but
the explanation is unconvincing. Newman, who was
not lacking insight on such matters, was more accurate in his suggestion that "vexation and anxiety
had much to do with his illness."[7]

By May 14 Lloyd was too weak to write. His wife,
Mary, constantly by the bedside, reported to Burton
that he was not better:

> He thinks himself very ill, and desires me to say that
> the subject of his letter to you has nothing to do
> with it, that he is not fretting, but suffering merely
> from bodily illness. He also desires me to beg that
> you will come to Town as he wishes to see you
> much. I shall be particularly glad to see you as soon
> as you can come, — for although he will not allow it
> now, I am convinced that fretting about some mat-
> ter, (though I don't [know] what they [sic] are) has
> much to do with his illness, but I shall be particular-
> ly obliged to you if you will not notice this, if you
> write again, nor say a word of it to any one.[8]

6. Lloyd to Burton, May 11, 1829, Shrewsbury School MS., I, fol. 85.

7. A. Mozley, *Letters and Correspondence of Newman*, I, 208.

8. Mrs. Mary H. Lloyd to Burton, May 14, 1829, Shrewsbury School
MS., I, fol. 86.

When Edward Copleston agreed on May 20 to sub-
stitute for Lloyd in delivering the episcopal charge
to ordinands at Oxford, the word circulated
throughout the University that the Bishop's "bilious
condition" was now uncontrollable. On May 26
young W.E. Gladstone heard that Lloyd was " most
alarmingly ill," and despite an erroneous report of
improvement in *Jackson's Oxford Journal*, Lloyd's
brother wrote to Burton on May 30 that the Bishop
was "in a very precarious state." London friends
checked anxiously and regularly with the doctors.
Throughout the night of May 30 three physicians
alternated at the bedside, all to no avail. On Sunday
afternoon, May 31, 1829, between 3 and 4 p.m.,
Lloyd breathed his last.[9]

To a private funeral in the chapel of Lincoln's Inn
only Peel, Burton, and John Saunders, Lloyd's
curate at Cuddesdon, were invited.[10] The body was
laid to rest in the sepulchre of Lincoln's Inn Chapel,
a fitting return to the place where Lloyd got his first
taste of public duty on the way towards his Oxford
professorship and bishopric. Shortly after the burial,
various friends debated the possibility of erecting a
monument, founding a theological prize, or creating
an Oxford scholarship in honor of the deceased; but
those schemes were abandoned in favor of an ornate

9. Edward Copleston to Burton, May 20,1829, Shrewsbury School MS.,
    I, fol. 88; Gladstone, *Diaries,* I, 243; *Jackson's Oxford Journal,* May 30,
    1829; W.F. Lloyd to Burton, May 30 and 31, 1829, Shrewsbury
    School MS., I, fols. 90-91; Churton, *Memoir of Joshua Watson,* I, 293;
    J.E. Denison to Burton, June 2, 1829, Shrewsbury School MS., I,
    fol. 92.

10. W.F. Lloyd to Burton, June 2,1829, Shrewsbury School MS., I, fol.
    93.

marble plaque under the great west window to the left of the entrance in the Oxford cathedral.[11] From Lloyd's private library Burton was given the Prayer Book in which his mentor had written marginal notes and references.[12] The remainder of the library, 1278 volumes in all, was sold by auction at Sotheby's in early July. At least one copy of the catalogue of that sale has survived,[13] shedding light on the quite remarkable collection of books which Lloyd possessed. Most of the volumes were eighteenth and early nineteenth century editions, ranging from the classics to philosophy, history, and theology. About 140 of the volumes, however, were seventeenth-century editions, and about 40 were published in the sixteenth century. The oldest was a 1502 edition of Sophocles' *Tragaediae Septum*. Interestingly present was a 1558 *Breviarum Romanum* and a 1552 *Book of Common Prayer* — the former selling for thirteen shillings and the latter for £1.13; there were no less than 21 editions of the *Novum Testamentum Graecum*. Lloyd's younger brother, William Forster, bought a large number of the books and Robert Isaac Wilberforce purchased several, passing one on to John Keble.[14] For Lloyd's family

11. Peel to Burton, June 18, 1829, Shrewsbury School MS., I, fol. 113; F. Baring to Burton, June 16, 1829, fol. 109; Note by Burton, June 19, 1829, fol. 112.

12. J. Russell to Burton, June 16, 1829, Shrewsbury School MS., I, fol. 110.

13. In the Widener Library, Harvard University: *Catalogue of the Very Valuable Classical, Theological, & Miscellaneous Library of the Late Right Rev. Charles Lloyd ... which will be Sold by Auction, by Mr. Sotheby and Son ...* (1829).

14. John Keble to W.I. Wilberforce, August 1, 1829, Keble College MS. 69.

the auction netted £1538.5.6.[15]

The family moved from Cuddesdon to Oxford, and subsequently appeared infrequently in the memoirs and notes of contemporaries. Young Gladstone called on Mrs. Lloyd in 1831 just before he finished Oxford and launched his political career.[16] Apparently Mrs. Lloyd stayed on at Oxford, in part, in order to see her daughters married well. One old don later recalled how the daughters were regularly to be seen with their mother at undergraduate parties, and how one of the daughters carried on a somewhat imaginative courtship with an Exeter College undergraduate — hanging a canary cage in the window of the drawing-room as a sign to her suitor that the way was clear for a visit.[17] The only son, Charles, became a Student of Christ Church in 1841, a Senior Student in 1858, and died unmarried in 1862.[18]

Lloyd's death threw open two coveted posts, a bishopric and a professorship. In accordance with Lloyd's own wishes, Burton succeeded him as Regius Professor of Divinity.[19] But the bishopric was a more thorny problem. The earliest rumors indicated that Thomas Gaisford would be nominated, but he refused.[20] Mrs. Arbuthnot, noting a conversation of June 8 with the Duke of Wellington, described

15. On the catalogue now in Widener Library, the auctioneer's secretary wrote in the margins the name of each purchaser, with the price of each object sold.

16. Gladstone, *Diaries*, I, 340.

17. Tuckwell, *Reminiscences of Oxford*, p. 135.

18. I am grateful to Dr. J.F.A. Mason for this information.

19. Thomas Gaisford to Burton, June 15, 1829, Shrewsbury School MS., I, fol. 108.

20. Ellenborough, *Political Diary*, II, 46-50.

the Prime Minister as "a great deal puzzled" over the choice. If "a very celebrated divine," like Lloyd, could not be found, then the nominee "shd be a man of family & a gentleman." As Wellington "burst forth into one of his tirades at the laziness and inefficiency" of the English aristocracy, he had a sympathetic listener in Mrs. Arbuthnot. It was "very true," she admitted, "that those men of family who go into the church think of getting livings and preferments but never of studying and making themselves fit for the dignities of the Church."[21] A man without an aristocratic heritage who had nevertheless proven himself as a scholar would be more acceptable than an aristocratic nonentity. But another Lloyd was not to be found. Finally the Prime Minister selected an aristocratic Christ Church man, Richard Bagot, the nephew of the Dean of Christ Church (Lewis Bagot) prior to Cyril Jackson.

Lloyd's reputation was as controversial in death as it had been in life. *The Standard*, erroneously reporting that the Bishop of Gloucester as well as the Bishop of Oxford died on May 31, noted simply and heartlessly that "the former was an honest man."[22]

21. H. Arbuthnot, *Journal*, II, 282.
22. *The Standard*, June 2, 1829. In the same issue *The Standard* announced its error concerning Christopher Bethell, the Bishop of Gloucester, who lived until 1859.

Soon thereafter an Anglican cleric and popular
writer, George Croly, heaped further scorn on the
memory of the Bishop of Oxford, whose altered
position on the Catholic question was one of "the
most painful features of the entire transaction."
Lloyd's hair-splitting "rambling declamation" on the
subject of idolatry was, to Croly, "the Romish principle" by which foul deeds were done under the guise
of sanctimonious terms. "The Athenian idolator
should have learned in the school of the Oxford
professor, and beaten St. Paul out of the field."
Recapitulating the derision of the press against
Lloyd, Croly mercilessly suggested that there was a
sense of retribution in the recent sequence of events
culminating in Lloyd's death: "No man can long re-
sist this storm, unless he find strength within. The
wretched prelate made no defence: he shrank from
the infliction; and in a single month from the time of
his fatal speech, the defender of idolatry was in his
grave."[23]

Lloyd's reputation, however, was not without defense. One able vindicator was Noel Ellison, a rector
in Somerset and late fellow and tutor of Balliol
College. Himself disappointed and perplexed by
Lloyd's recent support of the Catholics, Ellison
nevertheless insisted that the late bishop did not
merely turn his opinion "to the breeze" to engage in
"any thing like trickery, truckling, or time-serving"
in order to gain ecclesiastical promotion. His change
on the Catholic question was a mark of independen-
dence, not instability. For the integrity of his
character, according to Ellison, one should ask the

23. George Croly, *Life and Times of His Late Majesty, George the Fourth; with
    Anecdotes of Distinguished Persons of the Last Fifty Years* (New York,
    1831), pp. 355-57.

parishioners whom he served and the friends who knew him personally. Most of all, one should defer to the opinion of the young Oxford men who benefited from his personable instruction: "Go ask his pupils who found him 'the directing and controlling friend, as well as the official professor'."[24] The point was well made. In the final analysis Lloyd's primary importance lay not in his support of Catholic Emancipation, whatever his motives on that issue. The bill would have passed the House of Lords without his support. Nor is he memorable for anything he wrote. *The Monthly Magazine* noted accurately that he never "in the slightest degree, distinguished himself in the world of letters."[25] Certainly he was not a gifted administrator, and did not live long enough to learn how to handle the problems within the diocese of Oxford. His teaching was his strongest suit. Even his relation to Peel is best understood in the terms of a teacher-pupil relationship. Until the late 1820's Peel was forever deferential, never forgetting that Lloyd was his tutor, the first-among-equals on any matter touching scholarly subjects or Oxford politics. Only in 1828 and 1829 did Peel move ahead of Lloyd on issues concerning the relation of the Church to the State, and even then he was thrashing out his own position in correspondence with his mentor, building on Lloyd's arguments sufficiently to depart from and ultimately to contradict the principles he was being taught.[26] If a good teacher is one who, in addition to

24. Ellison, *Protestant Errors and Roman Catholic Truths,* pp. 209-11.

25. *The Monthly Magazine* (1829), p. 469.

26. See Olive J. Brose, *Church and Parliament: The Reshaping of the Church of England 1828-1860* (Stanford, 1959), p. 15.

imparting knowledge, inculcates self-confidence to
his pupils, then Lloyd was a good teacher indeed.
His students took what he had to offer, made it their
own, and proceeded to draw out new implications.

A good example was Newman, who traced the
basis of his discovery of the Catholic doctrine of
forgiveness to Lloyd's teachings. From his
Evangelical heritage Newman had long believed in
"the natural corruption of the heart, and the necessity of a change," but had never connected that
change with the sacrament of baptism. In hearing
Lloyd expound on the doctrine of regeneration as "a
mere opening of new prospects, when the old score
of offenses is wiped away, and a person is for the
second time put, as it were on his good behaviour,"
Newman suddenly saw the inadequacy of the Protestant conception of forgiveness. In his diary he wrote
in January, 1825: "It seems to me that the great
stand is to be made, *not* against those who deny a
spiritual change altogether."[27] Lloyd, old High
Churchman that he was, had imbibed the pale
Protestant view of baptism, a view which the more
mature Newman would dismiss as liberalism. On this
matter the teacher inadvertently served as a foil for
the pupil.

Lloyd's impact on Newman was admittedly in-
direct. His emphasis on exegetical criticism, historical research, and the external proofs of the
Christian religion did not appeal to one who was
more attuned to dogma, philosophy, and internal
evidence of faith. "He was not," Newman later
wrote, "the man to exert an intellectual influence
over Mr. Newman or to leave a mark upon his

27. Newman, *Autobiographical Writings*, p. 78.

mind."[28] It was Richard Whately, not Lloyd, who taught Newman to think critically and to reason sharply, "to see with my own eyes," in Newman's words, "and to walk with my own feet."[29]. But if Whately taught Newman to walk, Lloyd pushed him forward. His influence was personal and psychological, not philosophical. He assigned the budding young scholar work to do, and made him believe he could do it.[30] In fact Newman's leadership of the Tractarian Movement in the 1830's owed much to Lloyd, for though Newman remained essentially a reserved man, the inhibiting shyness which characterized his early days at Oxford was overcome in the rough but generous treatment by Lloyd. "He brought me forward, made me known, spoke well of me, and gave me confidence in myself," Newman acknowledged.[31]

This personal rather than dogmatic impact explains the total absence of any reference to Lloyd in the first chapter of Newman's *Apologia,* which was an explicit account of the early development of his religious *opinions.* Yet the memory of Lloyd lingered in Newman's mind. In defense of his "Tract 90" in 1841, he cited Lloyd as a predecessor who held that beneath the unpalatable forms of Romanism lay an essence of faith not unlike Anglicanism. And he quoted from Lloyd's article in *The British Critic* (1825), to show "that the Reformers did not aim at decrees or abstract dogmas, but against a living system, and a system which it is quite possible to

28. *Ibid.,* p. 71.
29. Newman, *Apologia,* p. 11.
30. Newman, *Autobiographical Writings,* pp. 72, 197.
31. A. Mozley, *Letters and Correspondence of Newman,* I, 209.

separate from the formal statements which have served to represent it."[32]

One other aspect of Lloyd's legacy, as far as Newman was concerned, lay in the latter's reverence for bishops. When Richard Bagot, still the Bishop of Oxford in 1841, reprimanded Newman for his views as expressed in "Tract 90," retirement to Littlemore and ultimately the flight to Rome formed a natural sequence of events. Newman's bishop was his Pope, the voice of God at the head of the visible Church. Though he claimed to have founded this view on the Epistle of St. Ignatius,[33] there is doubtless a great deal of truth in Thomas Mozley's suggestion that "from first to last he had the deepest reverence for Bishops as such, and the greatest dread of anything that might interfere with pleasant relations to them," because he had been "on very intimate terms with Lloyd" and had known in Lloyd a bishop whose intrinsic character blended with his external authority in commanding respect.[34]

With Edward Bouverie Pusey, the other great leader of the Oxford Movement, there is no question about the profound importance of Lloyd's work. In 1829 Pusey was thrown into a closer relationship with Newman, Froude, Keble, Palmer and the other leaders of the movement for theological and ecclesiastical revival in the 1830's. As a Tractarian, Pusey steered a course which perhaps would have perturbed his "guardian friend."[35] His increasingly

32. J.H. Newman, *A Letter Addressed to the Rev. R.W. Jelf ... in Explanation of No. 90, in the Series called The Tracts for the Times* (Oxford, 1841), pp. 10-11.

33. Newman, *Apologia*, p. 50.

34. T. Mozley, *Reminiscences of Oriel and the Oxford Movement*, II, 441.

35. Liddon, *Pusey*, I, 202.

isolationist approach to theology, centering in
Biblical studies and the ancient fathers to the ex-
clusion of modern criticism, was *not* what Lloyd sent
him to Germany for. Certainly Pusey's gloomy un-
willingness "to look at the beauty of nature without
inward confession," his resolve never to smile except
with children, and his morbid concern with the fires
of hell,[36] would have struck no responsive chord
whatsoever in his mentor. Nor can one imagine what
Lloyd would have done with Pusey's ascetic emphasis on fasting. The denial of good food and drink
was, to Lloyd, a diet — nothing more, nothing less.
Yet in Pusey's dedicated scholarly approach, his con-
centration on scriptural exegesis, his devotion to
traditional teachings, and his refusal ever to consider
forsaking his Anglican heritage, one sees Lloyd writ
large.

As Lloyd was the first person ever to publish *The
Book of Common Prayer* with red-lettered rubrics, it
was fitting that some of his most influential work was
done in the area of liturgical studies. Dean Church,
referring to Hurrell Foude's development, put the
matter well:

> Bishop Lloyd's lectures had taught him and others,
> to the surprise of many, that the familiar and
> venerated Prayer Book was but the reflexion of
> mediaeval and primitive devotion, still embodied in
> its Latin forms in the Roman Service books; and so
> indirectly had planted in their minds the idea of the
> historical connection, and in a very profound way
> the spiritual sympathy, of the modern with the pre-
> Reformation Church.[37]

36. See Battiscombe, *Keble*, p. 270.
37. Church, *Oxford Movement*, p. 47.

Froude's perspective on the liturgy, gathered from
Blanco White as well as Lloyd, was expressed in
"Tract 63."[38] His distrust of an Erastian politico-
ecclesiastical arrangement was in large measure connected with his dread of "some foul deterioration of
the Liturgy" at the hands of liberal reformers.[39]
Lloyd's teaching lay behind that concern.

Lloyd's copious notes in the wide margins of his
own Prayer Book, which was passed on to Edward
Burton and is now preserved in Christ Church
Library, reveal the perspective which mightily impressed young Oxford theologians of that generation. With lines such as "so in the Missal," "the same
as in the Missal," "the same as in the Missal — except
that. . .," he constantly emphasised the similarity of
the Prayer Book to the Roman Missal. Occasionally
he showed how the English Reformers changed the
wording of the old Breviary to suit their own views,
as in the tempered lines on fasting and abstinence in
the Collect for the first Sunday in Lent. Citing often
from the Salisbury Breviary, the liturgy of John
Chrysostom, a French Missal, and the Sarum Missal,
Lloyd compared the ancient liturgies not only with
the changes effected during the Edwardian
Reformation, but also with further minor alterations
after the Savoy Conference of 1661.

In 1832 these notes on the Prayer Book were incorporated in William Palmer's *Origines Liturgicae*.
Palmer had long entertained the possibility of writing a commentary on the English liturgy, and in

38. Froude, *Remains*, II, 383-423. For an analysis of the manner in which
    Froude's "liturgical conservatism had a radical impact" on the Ox-
    ford Movement, see Piers Brendon, *Hurrell Froude and the Oxford
    Movement* (1974), pp. 141-44.

39. See Baker, "Froude and the Reformers," pp. 250-53.

1829 came from Trinity College, Dublin, to Worcester College, Oxford, in order to study the subject. But upon finding Lloyd working on the topic, he abandoned it, knowing that Lloyd himself planned to publish a commentary. Lloyd's death revived Palmer's interest, particularly when Burton turned Lloyd's notes over to him. The *Origines Liturgicae* was divided into two parts, the first dealing with primitive liturgies and the second devoted to the "antiquities of the English Ritual." Primarily Palmer was attempting to show how the English Prayer Book was a product of 1500 years' development, and that "they who truly feel the calm and sublime elevation of our hymns and prayers, participate in the spirit of primitive devotion."[40] Thus elements of Lloyd's labors lived on, under another's name, sustaining, in Church's words, "that interest of Churchmen in the early devotional language of the Church."[41]

Throughout England Lloyd's views on the Prayer Book were transmitted in sermons and lectures. Late in the century W.J. Copeland remembered sitting in a classroom at Winchester under the mastership of Dr. George Moberly, one of the members of Lloyd's private class. While an undergraduate at Balliol College from 1823 to 1826, Moberly had been indelibly impressed with Lloyd's commentary on the English liturgy. When Moberly himself became headmaster of Winchester College (1835-1866), his

---

40. William Palmer, *Origines Liturgicae, or Antiquities of the English Ritual, and a Dissertation on Primitive Liturgies*, 2 vols. (Oxford, 1836, 2nd ed.), I, iv-v.

41. Church, *Oxford Movement*, p. 214; cf. J.H. Overton, *The English Church in the Nineteenth Century 1800-1833* (1894), p. 185; and Owen Chadwick, *The Mind of the Oxford Movement* (1960), p. 28.

own pupils "listened to lectures on the same subject, delivered probably in the self-same words (if not even in the self-same manner) from the notes which the Doctor had entered in his prayer book in imitation of the method adopted by Lloyd."[42]

Another imitator of his pedagogical style as well as his theological orientation was J.B. Mozley. Although Mozley did not arrive at Oxford until after Lloyd's death, he not only partook of the oral tradition concerning the late Regius Professor but also studied with Lloyd's protégé, Edward Burton. Thus when Mozley himself served as Oxford's Regius Professor of Divinity from 1871 to 1878, it was said that he delivered post-graduate lectures on the Old Testament "following the example of Dr. Lloyd."[43]

Several writers in the nineteenth century offered their conjectures on the position that Lloyd would have taken in relation to the Oxford Movement, that attempt in the 1830's and 1840's by Newman, Pusey, Keble, Froude, and their friends to awaken the Church of England to its divine origins and spiritual authority. From 1833 to 1841 ninety tracts were written extolling reverential piety, apostolic succession, and catholic teaching. Much controversy

42. Copeland, "History of the Oxford Movement" (Pusey House MS.), II, 73-74.

43. A. Mozley, Letters and Correspondence of Newman, I, 82 (f.n.).

ensued. Newman's conversion to Rome in 1845 was
merely the most dramatic of several events in which
orthodox English churchmen lamented the
Romanizing tendencies of the Tractarians.
Had he lived, would Lloyd have made a difference? According to one old High Churchman,
Edward Churton, Lloyd's early death robbed the
Church of England of a counsellor who "would have
exercised an invaluable influence in the times of difficulty which were soon to follow."[44] Not content
with such a veiled suggestion, another partisan, G.V.
Cox, asserted explicitly that the late Bishop of Oxford would have *"kept in check"* the piety and zeal of
those young men who had learned their theology
from his hands. As Cox saw it, Lloyd would have
channelled the energies of the Newmanites in the
direction of showing the superior claims of a scriptural and apostolic Protestantism over the pre-
tensions of Roman Catholicism.[45] W.E. Gladstone
too thought that Lloyd "might have acted powerfully
for good on the fortunes of the Church of England,
by guiding the energetic influences which his
teaching had done much to form."[46]

No doubt Lloyd would have refused to stand
quietly to the side, watching his students and friends
play havoc with an established system of theological
teachings and academic order. Although he would
have agreed with much that the Tractarians said and
wrote, he had "enough of the old Adam" in him, as
Mrs. Battiscombe said of George Moberly, "to make
him a shrewd and worldly-wise critic" of "the

44. Churton, *Memoir of Joshua Watson*, I, 294.
45. Cox, *Recollections of Oxford*, pp. 131-32.
46. W.E. Gladstone, *A Chapter of Autobiography* (1868), pp. 52-53.

catastrophic lack of common sense too often displayed by the Tractarian leaders."[47] Conjectures specifying his reaction, however, tell more about the theorists than they do about Lloyd. The manner in which he would have responded to the Tractarians is, for the historian, a moot question.

Certainly Lloyd was instrumental in planting the seeds of Tractarian thought and expression. There is no little truth in the assertion made by J.H. Philpot, a former member of Lloyd's private class and a critic of those fellow pupils who became Tractarians, that Lloyd's "leading share in the Tractarian movement, which otherwise might have run a very different course, has been too often overlooked."[48]

If one accepts Professor Chadwick's suggestion that the Oxford Movement was "more a movement of the heart than of the head," then in John Keble lies the key to understanding the inner origins of Tractarianism. Keble's concern for sanctity, the place of awe and mystery in religion, and the centrality of the conscience as the way to grow in holiness and to do one's duty, were emphases which supposedly marked the difference between the old-fashioned orthodox High Churchmen and the men of the Oxford Movement.[49] There is a tendency, however, to make the distinction too sharp between the matter of "heart" and "head," between the new and the old churchmanship in early nineteenth-century England. In truth, matters of belief and historical tradition were fundamental to the Tractarian frame of mind. Pusey's summary of Tractarian

47. Battiscombe, *Keble*, p. 183.
48. J.H. Philpot, *The Seceders (1829-1869)* (1930), p. 16.
49. See Chadwick, *Mind of the Oxford Movement*, pp. 11, 28.

teachings, enunciated in 1840, smacks of the old High Church tradition, with only a few emendations.[50] And this was the tradition that Lloyd brought alive to his pupils.

The first and ablest historian of the Oxford Movement, R.W. Church, voiced the usual view that "Bishop Lloyd, if he had lived, would have played a considerable part" in the movement. Technically accurate as he was, Church was misleading. For in fact Lloyd *did* play a considerable part in the movement — by awakening his students to the possibilities inherent in their heritage as well as in themselves. "But the influence of this learned theology was not equal to its value," according to Church: "Sound requires atmosphere; and there was as yet no atmosphere in the public mind in which the voice of this theology could be heard."[51] Such reasoning, however, can be reversed. The atmosphere provided by romantic sensibility, and the threat posed by Erastian reformists, would have produced little fruit had there not been a renewal of theological interest in the 1820's. If John Keble was the inspiration, then Charles Lloyd was the instructor of the Tractarians.

Those energetic young dons who participated in the Oxford Movement thrived on an enlivened veneration for ancient learning, a renewed commitment to the dialectical process of arriving at truth, and the unspoken assumption that tutors and undergraduates should be mutually engaged in the search for truth and goodness. Newman and his friends were, in the words of David Newsome, "an impressive generation, but an academic revolution

50. *Ibid.*, p. 28.
51. Church, *Oxford Movement*, pp. 11-12.

had enabled it to be so." The renaissance of Lloyd's era heralded the "second Reformation" of Newman's. "It might indeed be argued that Oxford could never have been the effective centre of such a religious movement, nor could its leaders have wielded the influence which they did, had not the University previously experienced an intellectual revival."[52]

The connection of the Oxford Movement with the University's academic revival suggests one of the several limitations of the reform in which Charles Lloyd participated. Oxford's exclusive, all-absorbing Anglican bias went unchanged in the early nineteenth century, an orientation that was merely reinforced by the Tractarian controversy. For several decades after Lloyd's time, Oxford remained a citadel of the interests and privileges of the Church of England. Until 1856 no young man could even matriculate at the University without subscribing to the Thirty-nine Articles.

Another limitation had to do with the narrowly classical curriculum which Lloyd and his contemporaries scarcely altered. It is a well-known fact that the University of London was founded in the 1820's not only as an antidote to the religious exclusiveness of Oxford and Cambridge, but also as an institution devoted to modern studies. Despite the numerous indictments of journalists, memoirists, and official commissions, Oxford's classical emphasis continued virtually unchanged until mid-century. Not until 1850 were the honors schools of Natural Sciences, and Law and History established.[53]

52. Newsome, *Parting of Friends*, pp. 62-63, 65.

53. See Llewellyn Woodward, *The Age of Reform 1815-1870* (Oxford, 1962), pp. 490-92.

Other features of Lloyd's Oxford which resembled
the past more than the future — such as the
autonomy of colleges to the detriment of larger
University interests, "closed" fellowships awarded
still on the basis of patronage rather than examinations, and the University's continuing involvement in
the nation's political life — have prompted Sheldon
Rothblatt to note that late-Georgian Oxford, like
Cambridge, "possessed a character and tone entirely
its own. It should not be regarded as a forerunner to
the mid-Victorian period, for the innovations were
undertaken in an entirely different spirit and for different reasons than were the greater changes of the
mid-19th century."[54] Still, the renewal of the inner
life of the University in the first three decades of the
nineteenth century formed the basis for those later
institutional alterations embarked upon by the Victorians. Had Lloyd and his contemporaries not committed themselves to serious teaching and intellectual engagement, questions concerning admission,
curriculum, and fellowships would have had little
meaning. Certainly the larger questions having to do
with the nature and purpose of the university had
their roots in Lloyd's pre-Victorian world.

In an article for *The Quarterly Review* in 1827,
young Charles Lyell considered the "State of the
Universities," observing that the recent alterations in
"the habits and the mental cultivation" at Oxford
laid the foundations for "the progress of future improvement." Honor was due "those enlightened in-
dividuals" who breathed life into "that series of decisive measures which has already renovated so large

---

54. Rothblatt, "The Student Sub-culture and the Examination System in
    Early 19th Century Oxbridge," in Stone (ed.), *The University in Socie-
    ty*, I, 303.

a portion of their ancient academical system." Lyell's conclusion forms a fitting epitaph for Lloyd's generation, and especially for Lloyd himself: "If, desponding for a moment, they look for encouragement in their career, they may cast back their eyes on the revolution accomplished by their own efforts, in the short space of the last thirty years; and reflect how comparatively insignificant are the obstacles still to be surmounted, while the results to be anticipated are far more splendid, and, in their influence on the national welfare, far more extensively important."[55]

Oxford's golden age of excellence and international reputation lay in the future. The obstacles were hardly insignificant, but the University proved to be remarkably adaptable to the pragmatic and egalitarian demands of a new age. Although Charles Lloyd would have been a stranger in Victorian Oxford, distinguished academics such as Benjamin Jowett, Mark Pattison, and T.H. Green were debtors to Lloyd and his kind.

---

55. [Charles Lyell], "State of the Universities," *The Quarterly Review,* XXXVI (1827), 268.

APPENDIX

CANONS OF CHRIST CHURCH, 1803-30

	Date of Installation	No. of Stall	Date of death or resignation
The Chapter in 1803			
†W *John Randolph	9 Sept. 1783	V	r. 1806
W *Edward Venables Vernon (Harcourt)	13 Oct. 1785	IV	r. 1807
James Burton	23 Mar. 1793	I	d. 30 June 1825
Robert Holmes	28 Apr. 1795	VII	r. 1804
W *Thomas Hay	6 June 1795	VIII	d. 29 Jan. 1830
W *William Jackson	2 Aug. 1799	III	r. 1815
W *Charles Henry Hall	30 Nov. 1799	II	r. 1807
† Joseph White	22 Apr. 1802	VI	d. 22 May 1814
The Succession of Canons, 1803-30			
William Howley	2 May 1804	VII	r. 1809
†W *Charles Henry Hall	16 Feb. 1807	V	r. 1809
W *Samuel Smith	10 Mar. 1807	II	r. 1824
W *Edward Christopher Dowdeswell	13 Feb. 1808	IV	d. 1 Aug. 1849
† William Howley	29 Nov. 1809	V	r. 1813
W *Frederick Barnes	17 Feb. 1810	VII	d. 19 Aug. 1859
† William Van Mildert	3 Nov. 1813	V	r. 1820
† Richard Laurence	20 June 1814	VI	r. 1822
W *Phineas Pett	19 Feb. 1816	III	d. 4 Feb. 1830
† Frodsham Hodson	7 Nov. 1820	V	d. 18 Jan. 1822
† *Charles Lloyd	20 Feb. 1822	V	d. 31 May 1829
† Alexander Nicoll	2 July 1822	VI	d. 24 Sept. 1828
*Henry Woodcock	19 Mar. 1824	II	d. 8 Aug. 1840
William Buckland	14 July 1825	I	r. 1845
† *Edward Bouverie Pusey	9 Dec. 1828	VI	d. 16 Sept. 1882
†W *Edward Burton	1 Aug. 1829	V	d. 19 Jan. 1836
*Richard William Jelf	15 Mar. 1830	VIII	d. 19 Oct. 1871
W *John Bull	15 Mar. 1830	III	d. 21 Feb. 1858

* *Gremial member of Christ Church*
† *University Professor*
W. *At Westminster School*

d. *Died*
r. *Resigned*

BIBLIOGRAPHY

I. UNPRINTED SOURCES

BIRMINGHAM ORATORY, Edgbaston, Birmingham
Several letters from Richard Hurrell Froude to his
father, Robert Froude, describing Lloyd's Oxford classes
in 1826.

BODLEIAN LIBRARY, Oxford
Oxford Diocesan Papers, particularly the bundle in ex-
cess of 100 items concerning the dispute between Bishop
Lloyd and the Vicar of Swalcliffe, 1827-1829; Parish
Register Transcripts of Ewelme, 1813-1900; Ordination
Papers. Oxford University archival records; Diary of
John Hill, Vice-Principal of St. Edmund Hall; and mis-
cellaneous Oxford manuscript letters.

BRITISH MUSEUM (now *Library),* London
Several letters from the Liverpool Papers and the Dropmore Papers concerning Lloyd; and several hundred letters from the voluminous correspondence between Lloyd
and Peel in the Peel Papers, 1813-1829.

BUCKINGHAMSHIRE COUNTY RECORD OFFICE,
Aylesbury
Parish Registers for West Wycombe and Bradenham,
and the Disbursement Book of Richard Levett.

CHRIST CHURCH, Oxford
The Correspondence of George Robert Chinnery (14
volumes), 1808-1811; Christ Church Caution Book,
1743-1804; Christ Church Collections Book, 1803-1806;
Christ Church Chapter Books, 1802-21 and 1822-35; Dr.
Lloyd's Private Accounts. All in Christ Church Archives.
Diary of J.J. Buxton, 1809, in Christ Church Library.

KEBLE COLLEGE, Oxford
Letters from Keble to friends, concerning Lloyd.

LAMBETH PALACE LIBRARY, London
Letters of Cyril Jackson and William Howley, pertaining
to Lloyd.

MAGDALEN COLLEGE, Oxford
Letters from Lloyd to Martin Routh, 1828.

PUSEY HOUSE, Oxford
Correspondence in the Pusey Papers between Pusey and
Lloyd, 1826-1828; Pusey and Richard Salwey,
1824-1827; R. W. Jelf and Pusey, 1827; and William
Howley to Lloyd, 1828. Also Canon H. P. Liddon's
manuscript record of a conversation with Cardinal J. H.
Newman, 1883. In the Copeland Papers is W. J.
Copeland's manuscript "History of the Oxford Move-
ment" (2 vols.), 1881; and in the Bagot Letters is a
helpful letter from F. E. Paget to Robert Eden, 1879.

SHREWSBURY SCHOOL, Shrewsbury
About a dozen letters from Lloyd to Edward Burton, and
several letters pertaining to Lloyd's death and legacy, in
the Burton Letters, vols. I-II.

II. PRINTED SOURCES

A. Newspapers and Periodicals

British Critic
Christian Guardian and Church of England Magazine
Edinburgh Review
Gentleman's Magazine
Jackson's Oxford Journal
Monthly Magazine
Morning Chronicle (London)
New Monthly Magazine and Literary Journal
Oxford University and City Herald
Quarterly Review
The Standard (London)
The Times

B. Books and Pamphlets

Acland, T. D., *Memoir and Letters of the Right Honourable Sir Thomas Dyke Acland,* ed. A. H. D. Acland, 1902.*

Allardyce, Alexander, ed., *Letters from and to Charles Kirkpatrick Sharpe,* 1888. 2 vols.

Arbuthnot, Charles, *The Correspondence of Charles Arbuthnot,* ed. Arthur Aspinall, 1941.

Arbuthnot, Harriet, *The Journal of Mrs. Arbuthnot 1820-1832,* eds. Francis Bamford and the Duke of Wellington, 1950. 2 vols.

Aspinall, Arthur, ed., *The Letters of King George IV, 1812-1830,* Cambridge, 1938.

————, ed., *Three Nineteenth Century Diaries,* 1952.

Barker, E. H., *Parriana; or Notices of the Rev. Samuel Parr,* 1838. 2 vols.

[Beste, H. D.], *Personal and Literary Memorials,* 1829.

[Blake, H. J. C.], *Reminiscences of Eton,* Chichester, 1831.

Boone, J. S., *The Oxford Spy, in Four Dialogues,* Oxford, 1819.

Burke, Edmund, *The Works of Edmund Burke,* 1894, 2 vols.

Churton, Edward, *Memoir of Joshua Watson,* 1861. 2 vols.

* All these books and pamphlets, like those secondary works in the next section of the bibliography, were published in London unless otherwise indicated.

Clinton, F. J. Fynes, *Literary Remains of Henry Fynes Clinton,* 1854.

Colchester, Charles Lord, ed., *The Diary and Corre-spondence of Charles Abbot, Lord Colchester,* 1861. 3 vols.

Coleridge, J.T. *A Memoir of the Rev. John Keble,* 1880.

Cox, G. V., *Recollections of Oxford,* 1868.

Creevey, Thomas, *The Creevey Papers,* ed. Herbert Maxwell, 1923.

Croker, J. W., *The Croker Papers: The Correspondence and Diaries of the Late Honourable John Wilson Croker,* 1844. 3 vols.

Croly, George, *Life and Times of His Late Majesty, George the Fourth; with Anecdotes of Distinguished Persons of the Last Fifty Years,* New York, 1831.

Denison, G. A., *Notes of My Life, 1805-1878,* 1878.

De Quincey, Thomas, *Memorials and Other Papers,* Boston, 1856. 2 vols.

Doyle, F. H., *Reminiscences and Opinions, 1813-1885,* 1886.

Ellison, Noel, *Protestant Errors and Roman Catholic Truths,* 1829.

An Enquiry into the Studies and Disciplines, adopted in the two English Universities, as preparatory to Holy Orders in the Established Church; in a Letter Respectfully Addressed to the Right Hon. Robert Peel, 1824.

Froude, R. H., *Remains of the Late Rev. Richard Hur-rell Froude* , [eds. John Keble and J. H. Newman], 1838-39. 4 vols.

Gaskell, C. M., ed., *An Eton Boy; being the Letters of James Milnes Gaskell from Eton and Oxford 1820-1830,* 1939.

Gibbon, Edward, *The Autobiography of Edward Gibbon,* 1920.

Gladstone, W. E., *A Chapter of Autobiography,* 1868.

———, *The Gladstone Diaries, Vol. I: 1825-1832,* ed. M.R.D. Foot, Oxford, 1968.

Charles Greville, *The Greville Memoirs, 1814-1860,* eds. Lytton Strachey and Roger Fulford, 1938. 8 vols.

Hansard's Parliamentary Debates, new series.

[Heber, Amelia], *The Life of Reginald Heber,* 1830, 2 vols.

Law, Edward, *Lord Ellenborough, A Political Diary, 1828-1830,* 1881. 2 vols.

Liddon, H. P., *Life of Edward Bouverie Pusey,* 1893-7. 4 vols.

Lloyd, Charles, ed., *The Formularies of Faith put forth by Authority during the Reign of Henry VIII,* Oxford, 1825.

McVicar, John, *The Early Life and Professional Years of Bishop Hobart,* Oxford, 1838.

Mozley, Anne, ed., *Letters and Correspondence of John Henry Newman during his Life in the English Church,* 1891, 2 vols.

Mozley, Thomas, *Reminiscences chiefly of Oriel College and the Oxford Movement,* 1882. 2 vols.

Newman, J. H., *Apologia Pro Vita Sua; being a History of his Religious Opinions,* 1883.

————, *Autobiographical Writings,* ed. and introd. Father Henry Tristram, New York, 1957.

————, *A Letter addressed to the Rev. R.W. Jelf . . . in Explanation of No. 90, in the series called the Tracts for the Times,* Oxford, 1841.

Palmer, William, *Origines Liturgicae, or Antiquities of the English Ritual, and a Dissertation on Primitive Liturgies,* Oxford, 1836 (2nd ed.). 2 vols.

Parker, C. S., *Sir Robert Peel from his Private Papers,* 1891-9. 3 vols.

Park , J. A., *Memoirs of the Late William Stevens,* 1859.

Peel, Robert, *Memoirs of the Right Honourable Sir Robert Peel, Part II: The Roman Catholic Question, 1828-9,* eds. Earl Stanhope and Edward Cardwell, 1857.

Pellew, George, *The Life and Correspondence of the Right Honourable Henry Addington, First Viscount Sidmouth,* 1847. 3 vols.

Pusey, E. B., *An Historical Enquiry into the Probable Causes of the Rationalist Character lately Predominant in the Theology of Germany,* 1828.

Quilller-Couch, L.M., ed., *Reminiscences of Oxford by Oxford Men, 1559-1850,* Oxford, 1892.

Rogers, Samuel, *Recollections of Samuel Rogers,* ed. "A. D.", 1856.

Rose, H. J., *The State of the Protestant Religion in Germany,* Cambridge, 1825.

Southey, Robert, *Letters from England by Don Manuel Alvarez Espriella*, 1808. 2 vols.

Schleiermacher, Friedrich, *A Critical Essay on the Gospel of St. Luke*, trans. and introd. Connop Thirlwall, 1825.

Stapylton, H. E., *The Eton School Lists, from 1791 to 1850*, 1854.

Taylor, Thomas, *Memoirs of the Life and Writings of the Right Reverend Reginald Heber, D.D., Late Bishop of Calcutta*, 1836 (3rd ed.), 2 vols.

Tuckwell, William, *Reminiscences of Oxford*, 1900.

Twiss, Horace, *The Public and Private Life of Lord Chancellor Eldon, with Selections from his Correspondence*, London and Philadelphia, 1844. 3 vols.

Van Mildert, William, *Sermons on Various Occasions, and Charges*, with a "Memoir of the Author" by Cornelius Ives, Oxford, 1838.

Vassal, H. R., Third Lord Holland, *Further Memoirs of the Whig Party 1807-1821 with some Miscellaneous Reminiscences*, ed. Lord Stavordale, New York, 1905.

[Ward, J. W.], *Letters of the Earl of Dudley to the Bishop of Llandaff*, 1840.

————, *Letters to "Ivy" from the First Earl of Dudley*, ed. E. H. Romilly, 1905.

Wordsworth, Charles, *Annals of My Early Life, 1806-1846*, 1891.

III. SECONDARY WORKS

Bagot, J. F., *George Canning and his Friends,* 1909. 2 vols.

Baker, W. J., "Henry Ryder of Gloucester, 1815-1824: England's First Evangelical Bishop," *Transactions of the Bristol and Gloucestershire Archaeological Society,* LXXXIX (1970), 130-44.

————, "Hurrell Froude and the Reformers," *Journal of Ecclesiastical History,* XXI, 3 (1970), 243-59.

————, "Julius Charles Hare: A Victorian Interpreter of Luther," *South Atlantic Quarterly,* LXX, 1 (1971), 88-101.

Best, G. F. A., "Church Parties and Charities: The Experience of Three American Visitors to England 1823-1824," *English Historical Review,* LXXVIII (1963), 243-62.

————, *Temporal Pillars: Queen Anne's Bounty, the Ecclesiastical Commissioners, and the Church of England,* Cambridge, 1964.

Bill, E. G. W., and J. F. A. Mason, *Christ Church and Reform 1850-1867,* Oxford, 1970.

Bourne, H. R. F., *English Newspapers: Chapters in the History of Journalism,* New York, 1966. 2 vols.

Boyer, C. B., *The History of the Calculus and its Conceptual Development,* New York, 1949.

Brendon, Piers, *Hurrell Froude and the Oxford Movement,* 1974.

Briggs, Asa, *The Age of Improvement 1783-1867,* 1959.

Brilioth, Yngve, *The Anglican Revival. Studies in the Oxford Movement,* 1925.

Brose, Olive J., *Church and Parliament: The Reshaping of Church of England 1828-1860,* Stanford, 1959.

Chadwick, Owen, *The Mind of the Oxford Movement,* 1960.

_____, *The Victorian Church,* Part I, 1966.

Church, R. W., *The Oxford Movement. Twelve Years 1833-1845,* 1892.

Clark, Andrew, ed., *The Colleges of Oxford; their History and Traditions,* 1892.

Clarke, M. L., *Greek Studies in England 1700-1830,* Cambridge, 1945.

Cook, E. T., *The Life of John Ruskin,* New York, 1911. 2 vols.

Dictionary of National Biography

Falkner, J. M., *A History of Oxfordshire,* 1899.

Feiling, Keith, *In Christ Church Hall,* 1960.

Gash, Norman, *Mr. Secretary Peel: The Life of Sir Robert Peel to 1830,* 1961.

_____, "Peel and the Oxford University Election of 1829," *Oxoniensia,* IV (1939), 162-73.

Green, V. H. H., *Oxford Common Room: A Study of Lincoln College and Mark Pattison,* 1957.

Halévy, Élie, *The Liberal Awakening 1815-1830,* trans. E. I. Watkin, New York, 1961.

Henriques, Ursula, *Religious Toleration in England 1787-1883,* Toronto, 1961.

Hiscock, W. G., *A Christ Church Miscellany,* Oxford, 1946.

Hollis, Christopher, *Eton, A History*, 1960.

Laprade, W. T., *England and the French Revolution, 1789-1797*, Baltimore, 1909.

McClatchey, Diana, *Oxfordshire Clergy 1777-1869: A Study of the Established Church and of the Role of its Clergy in Local Society*, Oxford, 1960.

Machin, G. I. T., *The Catholic Question in English Politics, 1820 to 1830*, Oxford, 1964.

Mack, E. C., *Public Schools and British Opinion 1780 to 1860*, 1938.

Mallet, C. E., *A History of the University of Oxford*, 1927. 3 vols.

Mathieson, W. L., *English Church Reform 1815-1869*, 1923.

Milman, Arthur, *Henry Hart Milman, D. D., Dean of St. Paul's: A Biographical Sketch*, 1900.

Newsome, David, *The Parting of Friends: A Study of the Wilberforces and Henry Manning*, 1966.

Overton, J. H., *The English Church in the Nineteenth Century 1800-1833*, 1894.

Pantin, W. A., *Oxford Life in Oxford Archives*, 1972.

Philpot, J. H., *The Seceders (1829-1869)*, 1930.

Reynolds, J. A., *The Catholic Emancipation Crisis in Ireland, 1823-1829*, New Haven, 1954.

Sheahan, J. J., *History and Topography of Buckinghamshire*, 1862.

Soloway, R. A., *Prelates and People: Ecclesiastical Social Thought in England 1783-1852*, 1969.

Stanley, A. P., *The Life and Correspondence of Thomas Arnold,* 1852.

Stone, Lawrence, ed., *The University in Society,* Princeton, 1974. 2 vols.

Sutherland, Dame Lucy, *The University of Oxford in the Eighteenth Century; a Reconsideration,* Oxford, 1973.

Thompson, H. L., *Christ Church,* 1900.

Ward, Mrs. Humphrey, *A Writer's Recollections,* New York, 1918. 2 vols.

Ward, Maisie, *Young Mr. Newman,* 1948.

Ward, W. R., *Georgian Oxford: University Politics in the Eighteenth Century,* Oxford, 1958.

————, *Victorian Oxford,* 1965.

Warre-Cornish, Francis, *The English Church in the Nineteenth Century,* 1910. 2 vols.

Watson, J. S., *The Reign of George III 1760-1815,* Oxford, 1960.

Welply, W. H., "George Chinnery, 1774-1852, with Some Account of his Family and Genealogy," *Notes and Queries* (January 29, 1927), 75-77.

Whitington, F. T., *Augustus Short, First Bishop of Adelaide,* 1888.

Winstanley, D. A., *The University of Cambridge in the 18th Century,* Cambridge, 1958.

Woodward, Llewellyn, *The Age of Reform 1815-1870,* Oxford, 1962.

Wordsworth, Christopher, *Scholae Academiae: Some Account of the Studies at the English Universities in the Eighteenth Century,* Cambridge, 1910.

INDEX